P.O.W.

One girl's experience in a Japanese P.O.W. camp

P.O.W.

One girl's experience in a Japanese P.O.W. camp

Gerarda Bossard

Hodder Moa Beckett

About the Author

Gerarda Bossard (nee Koning) came to New Zealand in 1960 after several years living in Australia and The Netherlands. This is her account of life in a Japanese concentration camp in the Dutch East Indies during World War II. Gerarda turned 71 in March 1999. She lives in Auckland with husband Oliver.

ISBN 1-86958-732-4

Published in 1999 by Hodder Moa Beckett Publishers Limited,
[a member of the Hodder Headline Group]
4 Whetu Place, Mairangi Bay, Auckland, New Zealand

Designed and produced by Hodder Moa Beckett Publishers Ltd
Printed by Griffin Press Pty Ltd, Australia

In loving memory of my parents
Louisa (1903-1996) and
Reijer (1901-1998).

Their love and great inner strength
sustained me during very difficult
times. With all my love.

God grant me the serenity to accept
the things I cannot change, courage
to change the things I can and the
wisdom to know the difference.

Acknowledgements

I wish to thank my husband, Oliver, for his support and patience – without it I could not have written my memoirs.

I wish to thank Geoff Young for his hard work in putting this book together. Thanks, Geoff. I believe your writing skills have helped produce a special book.

I am also grateful to my publishers, Hodder Moa Beckett, for bringing it all about.

Contents

Foreword ... 9
1. Threat to Innocence ... 11
2. A Colonial Family ... 13
3. Thorns in the Bed of Roses ... 21
4. Home Away From Home ... 25
5. Enemy at the Door ... 29
6. Rumours of My Death ... 33
7. Showing Respect ... 35
8. Illness and Death ... 41
9. Leaving Malino ... 45
10. Kampili ... 49
11. Acclimatisation ... 53
12. The Central Kitchen ... 57
13. The Boss ... 59
14. Daily Life ... 63
15. The Appendectomy ... 67
16. Mamma's Illness ... 73
17. The Pests ... 77
18. Terror from the Air ... 81
19. Weather Woes ... 83
20. Japanese Nerves ... 89
21. Light Relief ... 93
22. The New Year ... 95
23. Beautiful Night Skies ... 107
24. The Pits ... 109
25. Trench Warfare ... 111
26. Unable to Cope ... 115
27. Dogfights Above Kampili ... 119
28. 1944 – The Year of Death ... 121
29. From Bad to Worse ... 125
30. Mad Dogs ... 129
31. The Grind Goes On ... 131
32. Praying for Leida ... 135
33. Shattered Beliefs ... 137

34. Droning Nightmare 141
35. They Were Our Friends 143
36. The Inferno 147
37. Puppets of Propaganda 153
38. Boskamp 155
39. Execution Day 159
40. Peace at Last 163
41. Lingering On 165
42. The Lists 167
43. A Plane Comes in Peace 169
44. Farewell Boskamp, Hello Again to Kampili 173
45. Freedom at Last 177
46. Reunited at Last 183
47. Struggle for Normality 187
48. Bok'eh's Court Martial 189
49. Battles in the Peace 193
Epilogue 205

Foreword

Although what I am writing about happened more than 50 years ago when I was a teenager called Gerarda Koning, I cannot forget it. It still haunts me. Everything I relate happened between December 1941, when I was 13, and the end of October 1945. Our family was separated for nearly four years and our lives were completely disrupted and changed forever.

Myself, my mother Louisa and sisters Leida – then 15 – and Lia (4) were held by the Japanese at a concentration camp called Kampili on the Indonesian island of Sulawesi (then called Celebes) during World War II. Our father, who was mobilised in December 1941, was a prisoner in Makassar and then Batavia, now Jakarta. We didn't know whether we would see him again.

Our cosy world fell apart. I want to write about how we suffered physically, emotionally and psychologically, which affected us for many years and up to a certain degree, it still affects me.

There was the uncertainty of not knowing what was going to happen to us from day to day. At Kampili we were completely isolated. We were forced to live in abject poverty in the most primitive circumstances and our lives were put in grave danger as our Japanese captors had not marked our camp for identification by the Allied powers. The Japanese had ammunition depots, an airfield and a great number of troops close to our camp. We were sitting ducks.

We had no voice. We were totally at the mercy of the Japanese, who were so alien to us and who did not give us time and the opportunity to understand them. They were strange ugly little men who were armed, while we were defenseless women and children. They treated us with contempt and brutal force and made us perform heavy manual work and work for their war effort.

We were unable to read, although we had little time for that as we had to work most of the time. We had no reticulated water supply – only wells which would run dry – sewerage, drainage, furniture or bedding. All we had was the bare flimsy bamboo structures on a dirt floor.

Although I was a teenager, I had to become an adult almost overnight. There was no time to grow up naturally and gracefully. I had to spend the best years of my life as a prisoner of war. We were worked like slaves, mostly in the tropical sun which ruined my fair skin.

I was always hungry. I was very ill and I suffered bad headaches almost all the time.

With the passing of the years my memory has become sharper. It is like looking at a video. All the people, the camp, the cruel camp commandant, the events like the horrendous aerial bombardment of our camp resulting in an horrific inferno, are all very clear now.

Because we were living so close together with no privacy, we shared the grief, anxiety, stress and distress of others as well as our own. There were people who could not cope but there were always others who were strong and able to help them.

I want to pay tribute to all those beautiful and courageous people who endured so much hardship with such dignity and good spirit and helped me endure the hardships and survive.

I want to pay a special tribute to the heroine who wrestled a rabid dog with her bare hands and held it by the throat so that other women could kill it without being bitten. She was bitten and died a horrible death. She deserved a posthumous medal of valour; I also laud those dedicated teachers who, against the odds and under very difficult circumstances, still managed to teach us.

Many of these beautiful people have passed away but I shall always remember them, even though I cannot remember all their names.

Gerarda Bossard
25 January 1999

1. Threat to Innocence

I probably would have killed myself if I had been raped. I was 15 and petrified and that was my constant fear after Mamma and the other mothers had refused the commandant's desire for the teenage girls to be taken as "entertainment" girls for the Japanese officers.

The commandant had been ordered by his superiors to supply some girls from our camp and Mrs Joustra, our leader, told Mamma, who was disgusted. "No. There is no way Leida and Gerda are going to be the Japs' playthings," Mamma said and she was backed up by the other mothers.

I was innocent but I knew exactly what "entertainment" girls were forced to do and I was sick at the thought. What really happened, I don't know, but Leida and I weren't taken away and I don't think anybody else was either.

What I do know is that we would have been forced to be the Japanese officers' whores if it wasn't for the stand taken by our courageous mothers. They would never have let us go and luckily their resolve was not put to the test.

Maybe the Japs found some women who volunteered or perhaps they forced some of the poor native girls in Makassar to entertain them. We never found out but the horrible suggestion was not mentioned again.

I was always scared and I made sure I was never on my own at any time. I was always close to people, in particular adults. This threat from the repulsive commandant made me very nervous and uneasy because I was afraid the Japs could still take us away at any time. We were, after all, their prisoners.

2. A Colonial Family

Pappa would have liked to be a doctor and to study at the medical school in the Dutch city of Leiden. He would have made a very good doctor but his father could not afford it. Instead he studied at an agricultural college, got a diploma in horticulture, went to work in a rose nursery and became interested in horticulture.

At this time he read an advertisement in a newspaper seeking young men interested in a career in the postal services in the Dutch East Indies. They were to enroll in the Postal School in Leiden to study the course which would qualify them to secure a job in the Asian colonies. Pappa was interested, enrolled and successfully completed the course and passed the exams.

During his stay and studies in Leiden he met Mamma. She was born in Leiden in 1903, two years after Pappa. They fell in love and were married on

July 15 1925. Three days later they sailed to their new country.

Pappa's first post was at Semarang on Java's north coast but he was there only a short time before he was transferred to Soerabaja, where both Leida and I were born. Leida arrived on April 26, 1926 and I on March 12, 1928.

Pappa was transferred again in 1928 and with two babies they had to travel to Palembang in east Sumatra. He worked there for two years before being posted to Batavia (Jakarta). Here our neighbours were the family Janke and Leida and I called them Oom Walter and Tante Katie. They had an adult daughter called Mona and then there was Tante Katie's brother we called Oom Eddie.

The time we lived in Batavia was very pleasant and we often went to the beach for a swim, where Leida and me loved playing in the shallow waves or on the black beach sand.

Oom Walter was a talented musician. Not only could he play almost any musical instrument, he could also build pianos and organs including pipe organs for churches. Years later Oom Walter built a beautiful piano for me.

But we had to say goodbye again. In 1931 Pappa got his eight month leave – common at that time – and we sailed to Holland, where we stayed with Mamma's relatives in Leiden. While we were living in Holland, Mamma and Pappa took Leida and I to meet Pappa's relatives.

When we went back to the Dutch East Indies, Pappa was posted to Bandoeng in Central West Java, a lovely city at that time with a pleasant climate. Mamma and Pappa had to set up house again and employ servants but this posting turned out to be a long one, so the job was not fraught with the same problems a temporary posting always posed.

We as a family tramped on the Tangkoeban Prahoe, a mountain the shape of a boat lying upside down. The scenery was beautiful and there were bungalows on the mountain slopes where one could stay overnight. Although I was only five, Pappa said I would climb for quite a distance before he would take me on his shoulders and carry on. Leida, being older, tramped happily till the party stopped for a rest.

Leida and I went to school. We had three cats and Leida and I often had them in our beds, which Mamma did not like.

We had nice servants too. A man, a cook, a gardener and a woman to do the washing and ironing, clean the bedrooms and make the beds. Pappa always managed to have a beautiful garden with many colourful flowers. His favourites were orchids and one orchid only flowered at night under a full moon. Pappa would be watching and he would get us out of bed in the middle of the night to witness the beautiful graceful orchid bloom opening.

The houses in the Dutch East Indies usually had some rooms in the back part of the house where some of the servants lived. Mamma and Pappa always tried to employ a man and his wife who would live on the premises. Our servants were always nice to Leida and me, and we were nice to them.

Pappa had no car and he rode a bicycle to work, while Leida and I walked to school. When the rain was bucketing down our man servant had to get a demmo – a kind of taxi on three wheels – or a sado, a horse-drawn square type of buggy with black blinds on three sides which were let down when it rained.

Our family doctor was Dr Staal, who was a really good friend to us. He was living in a big house with beautiful things and polished parquet floors. He had no daughters and sometimes on a Sunday he would come in his car to pick up Leida and me and take us to the swimming pool. After some time playing and splashing in the glorious cool water, while the good doctor sat in a comfortable chair to keep an eye on us, Leida and I were treated to something nice to eat – usually involving ice-cream.

One day Leida fell very ill. She was screaming with pain in her tummy and Dr Staal came and laid Leida gently on the back seat of his car and drove her to the hospital. Leida had acute appendicitis and was operated on immediately. I felt lost and lonely and did not know what to do. Even the cats sensed something was wrong because they always kept close to me.

But Leida came home again and was soon back to normal. We were healthy girls and Mamma always insisted we ate good food, which included brown bread, fresh fruit and vegetables. We also had to drink milk. Every day Mamma made us take calcium in powder form and it tasted ghastly, but in later years I thanked my lucky stars for Mamma's good sense.

In 1938 Pappa was due for his second big leave. But in 1937, when Mamma was seven months pregnant with Lia, she wanted to go to Holland to give birth. Dr Staal did no want her to travel at that late stage but Mamma insisted.

Mamma, Leida and I sailed away, leaving Pappa behind to join us the following year. We had to say goodbye to Pappa, our servants and pets. The cats were going to a good home and Pappa was going to live with good friends.

Leida and I did not really like going to Holland. In Leiden we stayed with Mamma's parents and unmarried sister and we had to go to school and hated it.

The school was in the middle of the city and children speaking in a strange twang asked us how we could walk in shoes. They had been told that in the Dutch East Indies people did not wear shoes because they were too poor to buy them. We did not like the children or the teachers and Leida and I were bored stiff with school because we were ahead in all subjects.

Mamma's only sister, Tante Corrie, had a black piano which she never played and I longed to be able to play. It was agreed that I could take lessons and practise on Tante Corrie's piano.

Mamma took me to Miss Bakker, a spinster who lived with her spinster sister in an old-fashioned house. She was very kind and a good teacher.

The sisters had a housemaid, an antique car and a chauffeur. The car was large, square and very heavy and it had big square lights on the front and back. Occasionally I was invited to ride with the two Bakker sisters with the chauffeur wearing a beautiful uniform. The car was high off the ground and I could only just manage to climb aboard. Driving through Leiden in this unusual vehicle drew plenty of attention. People would stop in the street, staring at it and us, and I felt as if I was sitting in a cage in a zoo.

Oma, Opa and Tante Corrie were very nice to us but what I hated most was having to kiss Opa who had a prickly beard and moustache. Tante's little old dog, Foxie, did not like us and always snarled at us. It slept most of the day by the fire on a pillow in its wooden bed.

On June 16, 1937, we were told that we had a little sister. Tante Corrie took us to the hospital to see Mamma and the new arrival. Leida and I were disappointed as the baby shown to us looked like a furless rabbit. Mamma decided to call her Lia, short for Cornelia.

The family house in Leiden was now too small, so Mamma rented a house not far from her parents. We were allowed to take the piano with us so I could continue my piano lessons. Mamma employed an Indonesian woman to help her with the house chores and look after Leida and me. She had her hands full with baby Lia.

Tjitro, the servant, was a lovely person and just like a second mother to us. Although Mamma wanted her to eat with us in the dining-room, she refused and preferred to eat alone in the kitchen where it was always warm.

Mamma, who had relatives in Rotterdam, decided to go for a short visit. Tjitro was more than capable of looking after the three of us. We loved her and she always spoiled us rotten. Mamma packed a small suitcase which Tjitro insisted on carrying for her to the tramstop very close to home.

The suitcase wasn't heavy and as we were walking to the tramstop a man on a bicycle pedalled up to us, got off his bike and shouted to Mamma: "You bloody lazy bitch. Carry that suitcase yourself. That little woman is too old to carry it." Mamma replied calmly: "Mind your own business." Tjitro, not understanding, asked Mamma what the man said and when she was told she was disgusted. Tjitro would never dream of letting Mamma carry her own suitcase. The man was obliged to get on his bike and ride away.

A Colonial Family

Pappa came the following year when Lia was almost a year old. We had a nice family life again.

Since we had left him, Pappa had developed a growth near one ear and it seemed to grow and change colour and looked like an over-ripe strawberry. Pappa went to the doctor, who told him it should be removed and a short time later Pappa arrived home with a white bandage around his head like a turban. The over-ripe strawberry had been surgically removed as the thing had a root which was growing and would have played havoc in Pappa's head and could easily have killed him.

When Pappa's leave was up, he was notified that his next posting was Padang on Sumatra's west coast. Leida and I were pleased to leave Holland. It was too crowded and the people seemed like real busy-bodies. It was very hard to say goodbye to the lovely Tjitro. She wanted to come with us and we would have all liked nothing better but she had a contract with a company in The Hague to work with families on leave from the Dutch East Indies. So poor Tjitro had to return to The Hague, where her employers would find her another temporary job. We cried our eyes out and our sea voyage was marred by our grief. It was the same grief as one for a loved-one's death. We knew we would never see her again. We also felt sorry to say goodbye to our grandparents and aunt.

We disembarked at Medan on Sumatra's north-east coast. Pappa hired a taxi to drive to Padang. It was a square car with a rubber ball fixed just outside the car on the driver's side, which was in fact a car-horn and the driver squeezed it a lot on the journey.

We drove through some of the most beautiful scenery on Sumatra. On the first night we stayed in Prapat on the shores of Lake Toba, a huge stretch of blue water. In the centre of the lake was the island of Samosir. It was very hot weather and we felt rather uncomfortable.

The second night we spent in a pasanggrahan, a kind of resthouse, in a tiny place called Padangsidempuan and although there was so much natural beauty around us, we were very pleased to reach Padang.

Pappa rented a nice house with a big garden on the Simpang Haroe, a street on the outskirts of Padang. Pappa and Mamma had to furnish the house and employ servants, and Leida and I had to go to school. We also took an old dog, a bitch called Bruno, from people who were going back to Holland.

Pappa and Mamma wrote to Oom Walter in Batavia asking him to build a piano for me. Mamma and Pappa would have liked Leida to have learned the piano too but she wasn't interested.

The new piano arrived after some time and what a beauty it was. I was thrilled to bits. We found a good teacher and I had lessons again. That piano was my pride and joy. The case was made of blond native wood and the best and most important part was the sound board. My piano had the most beautiful and pure tone, it was worth every cent Mamma and Pappa paid Oom Walter.

Pappa also presented Leida and me with a second-hand bicycle each so we could bike to school, which was quite a long way from home.

I loved school. Because of the hot weather we had lessons from early morning till 1pm. I had a young Dutch teacher who had studied horticulture and after school in the afternoon he often took us on a walk and taught us the names and particulars of the different trees and plants. We carried a tin with us to collect plant samples which we put in our books later. He also kept an eye on us children while swimming in the large local swimming pool. This nice young man engaged in these activities voluntarily.

One day a little monkey turned up in our garden. It was sitting on Bruno the dog back to front and playing with Bruno's tail and using it like a bridle. Bruno, who had a lovely nature, didn't mind and as the monkey did not seem to belong to anyone, we kept it and called it Keesie.

She was like a little human being. She liked to do the washing in a bowl with soapwater and a piece of cloth. She rubbed the cloth between her two tiny hands, while grinning at us with pleasure. At meal times Keesie would sit with us at the table. If we were eating fruit a little hand would quickly snatch the morsel out of our hands. The rest of our menagerie were hens and doves. The doves were pretty little birds, beige in colour with a black band around their tiny necks.

Bruno got pregnant and gave birth to four healthy puppies and she was a very proud mother. We enjoyed watching Bruno and her rapidly growing family but we could not keep them and had to find four homes for the dogs.

Every now and then an earthquake would shake the ground. We always ran outside in the open, well away from the house and power lines. The ground would roll in waves under our feet. The tree crowns would wave in a most peculiar way, most unlike waving in the wind. Fortunately there were no serious quakes in our time at Padang and only minor damage was ever reported.

The scenery around Padang was magnificent, with dense forests and high mountains in the distance. Pappa, Leida and I would sometimes make trips on our bikes. One such trip was to a waterfall with our togs and picnic lunch. Mamma stayed home with Lia, who was still too young for bike trips. We loved that waterfall, splashing around in the cold, crystal clear water which cascaded down the hillside. We used to go tramping in those wonderful hills as well and life was very active and a lot of fun.

When we needed new dresses, Mamma bought materials and patterns and hired a male dressmaker. He deftly cut out the garments and sewed them on Mamma's Singer hand sewing machine, while he sat in the lotus position on a mat on the front verandah. I watched him in awe as he worked. He had a very long nail of the little finger on his right hand and with this he scratched seams open. Leida was very interested because she wanted to become a dressmaker when she grew up.

At this time I was suffering dreadful headaches. The doctor said that I was a typical European child and that the hot tropical climate was bad for my health. Mamma and Pappa decided I should be taken into the cool clear mountain air during the school holidays.

Mamma, Leida and I travelled by train to Fort de Kock (now called Bukittinggi), high up in the mountains. We stayed there in a hotel and Pappa would come up whenever he could get a few days off. The train ride always fascinated us. Part of the route went over a very high bridge through the Kloof van Harau, a tremendously deep and wide gap, flanked by steep rocky mountains reaching up to the sky, as we children described it. The floor of the chasm was covered with dense forests, huge age-old trees and even some palm trees were growing there. It was always green in the Kloof van Harau as it rained a lot there.

It was in Padang and Fort de Kock that I first became aware of Japanese men. Padang attracted many Japanese visitors and we thought they were tourists because they always carried cameras with which they took pictures of buildings, bridges and roads. At Fort de Kock the Japanese men also took many pictures.

They stayed at our hotel but kept very much to themselves. They never communicated with us and we were not deemed worthy enough for a polite greeting. In the dining room they would sit together and talk in their foreign tongue and after they had finished eating, would get their toothpicks out and openly pick their teeth. Very odd behaviour to someone who had been taught that to pick one's teeth in company was extremely bad manners. The teethpicking ritual was followed by loud belching – one after the other. How very rude, I thought, and as I looked at them they took no notice of anybody else in the room.

I thought that all the mothers of these men had not taught them very good manners. They had no shame, while we were very embarrassed. Little did we know that a Japanese belch is a compliment to the chef, although how the cook was supposed to know I have little idea.

Pappa had noticed on a number of occasions that these toothpicking belchers were taking an unusually large number of pictures. Pappa said he did not trust them and believed they were taking all the pictures for a purpose. He believed they were reconnoitring for the Japanese government. He did not like it and he proved to be right.

But that was all in the future. After a stay in lovely Bukittinggi, despite the toothpicking, belching Japanese in their black suits, I returned to hot Padang and was alright for a while before the headaches returned.

Bruno was already an old dog when we got her and after a while she started going blind. The vet said her eyesight problems were inoperable and this saddened us very much.

In 1941 Pappa was told he was being transferred to Makassar on the island of Celebes and we were told we couldn't take Bruno with us because of the risk of rabies.

Poor Bruno was now completely blind and we had to guide her everywhere. Mamma and Pappa set out to find her a good home, without success. Nobody wanted a blind dog and giving her to the natives would have resulted in poor old Bruno probably being neglected and starving to death, so Pappa had a serious talk with the vet. He talked to Pappa in a very friendly and understanding way. He hated putting animals down but for Bruno it was the kindest way. So the difficult decision was made to put Bruno to sleep and this time it was even harder to say goodbye to our best friend. Leida and I cried for days. Pappa never really got over it, either, although we know it was the best thing to do, especially with the Japanese on the verge of invading the Dutch East Indies.

Our dressmaker friend was fond of Keesie, so he took the little monkey home with him. Most of our hens had died of a contagious infection and the few still alive were given good homes. Mamma and Pappa sold all the furniture and household goods which we could not take with us but my piano was not sold but packed in a large wooden crate and shipped to Makassar together with our personal baggage.

We sailed from Padang's Emma Haven to Batavia on Java, where we briefly met our good friends the Janke family again. From Batavia we travelled by train to Soerabaja, the capital of East Java and from there we sailed to Makassar.

In Makassar we stayed in a hotel till Pappa had found and rented a suitable house. They had to furnish it and had to employ servants. Pappa went to work at the Post Office and Leida and I went to school.

We had only lived there for a very short time and fortunately had not had the time to acquire any animals when the war broke out and life changed forever.

3. Thorns in the Bed of Roses

Things were so good for our family in 1941, one of the hundreds of Dutch families living in the colony of the Dutch East Indies, now Indonesia. Pappa worked for the postal service and had recently transferred to Makassar, now called Ujang Padang, on the island of Celebes (Sulawesi).

We lived in a nice rented house with a well-kept garden. We had four very nice Indonesian servants who did all the housework, cooking and gardening. Pappa paid them well and life was a bed of roses for us all.

I felt happy and secure. I loved school and was looking forward to going to the Hogere Burgerschool (high school). I had a beautiful piano specially built for me by a talented German friend of the family we called Uncle Walter. I was taking lessons and loved playing this much-treasured piano. I also loved reading and there were always plenty of books in the house as Pappa was also an avid reader. Leida and I each owned a brand new bicycle – a real treat in those days.

But life for our close-knit colonial family was soon to be shattered.

We were aware of the war in Europe but it all seemed so far away from our peaceful existence. Then came ominous rumblings and frightening rumours. It started when letters from friends and relatives in Holland stopped arriving. Pappa, Mamma and their acquaintances began looking grim and were unhappy. They told Leida and me that Germany had invaded Holland.

For a time, life went on as before, but there was a pervading mood of gloom with the adults always taking about war. At that time I did not really understand what war meant.

Then, on December 7, 1941, we heard that the Japanese had attacked Pearl Harbor, bringing the Americans into the war. The next day The Netherlands declared war on Japan. The war was now very close to home.

Some people had bomb shelters dug in their gardens as Japanese aircraft soon made their appearance and there were frequent air raids. A strict blackout was enforced and shades were placed over lamps in the houses. This naturally added to the gloom and doom which had descended on us.

On December 9, all able-bodied men were mobilised. Pappa appeared in a green army uniform looking very strange indeed. A Japanese invasion was imminent.

We did not have an air raid shelter and were invited to share one with one of Pappa's colleagues who, with his wife, lived close by. We children called them Oom (uncle) Henk and Tante (aunt) Dora.

The house next door to this charming, childless couple was empty except for the houseboy and the family pet dog. The husband had gone to join the army after sending his wife and children to Java, thinking it would be safer over there.

The dog, a Chow-Chow, was a nervous and frightened little creature which howled hysterically every time the air raid sirens screamed. We took the dog home with us and he slept under my bed and became very protective of me. I became very attached to my four-legged friend. I took him for walks three times a day after the school had been closed. I missed school terribly, but my little friend made up for the enforced holiday and the whole family grew very fond of him.

But like many things in those days, pleasures were not to last. One day the houseboy came to fetch him because his owner wanted to take him away with him. I was devastated and it was very sad to say goodbye. But that was only the beginning. We were to know greater sadness.

On January 20, 1942, news reached us that a Japanese fleet was sailing in the direction of Makassar, so the authorities were to evacuate the European women and children to Malino, a holiday resort in the mountains about 70km east of the city.

Some men sent their wives and children to Australia, while others sent theirs to the 'safe haven' of Java. Pappa wanted Mamma, Leida, Lia and me to go on the boat to Australia, but Mamma refused.

"No way," she said emphatically. "You have to stay, so the girls and I will stay too." And that was that. Mamma was always very determined. We stayed and despite everything that happened to us we did not regret Mamma's decision.

But we had to leave Pappa, which was incredibly hard. The authorities evacuated us to Malino, telling us not to take much luggage because, with much undue bravado and naivety, they expected us to be able to return to our homes in Makassar in about three weeks when they were sure they would have defeated the Japanese invaders.

Mamma packed one suitcase for the four of us. She always carried her large leather handbag wherever she went. She stuffed all the important papers and her and Pappa's wedding rings in it. The bag was bulging, but this bag which contained everything of importance regarding our identity, survived the war. Little else did.

I insisted on taking my own tiny suitcase in which I crammed a toothbrush, toothpaste, one dress, a pair of shoes and my watch and small items of importance to a 13-soon to be 14-year-old.

The next day we went with Tante Dora in her car because we did not own one. An Indonesian driver was assigned to each car and we were to be dropped at our assigned accommodation in Malino. After delivering the evacuees, the cars were immobilised.

Saying goodbye to Pappa was horrible, even though we were assured it would be for only a short time. It was distressing to see Pappa's slight figure in his green uniform become smaller and smaller as we drove away. Pappa had to defend the post office where he worked, but we hoped to be united again in a matter of weeks.

As it turned out, we never saw Pappa until October 1945.

4. Home Away From Home

The journey from Makassar to Malino was a hair-raising experience. The scenery was magnificent with the grandiose beauty of the mountains covered with majestic trees. On one side there were magnificent forests and on the other, steep, fathomless ravines which were also covered with dense forest. We felt very privileged indeed to live in such a beautiful country being surrounded by those pristine landscapes and age-old virgin rainforests.

But after a short time it was apparent that our Indonesian driver was inexperienced at driving on such roads. We could not enjoy nature's finest creations to the full extent because we had just left Pappa behind and because of the poor man's unsafe driving. He almost drove us off the road and finally, with the car teetering on the edge of a precipice Tante Dora took over and the journey became more bearable, despite the heat.

We were relieved when we finally arrived at our home away from home in Malino, the holiday bungalow of a Chinese doctor. The house was small but comfortable for a small family, but it had to house 17 people at once and many more later.

When we arrived the few bedrooms were already occupied, which left us the lounge/dining room. I had to sleep on a two-seater settee, which was uncomfortable as I could not stretch my legs. At night everybody would sit in this room and I would not be able to go to sleep until everybody else had gone to bed. I sure missed my own spacious bedroom and my comfortable bed with the neat kelambu (mosquito net), but I had to manage. I had to get used to communal living in a big way.

We were a mixed group of people in that house. The biggest bedroom was occupied by a Russian man and his wife and three small sons. I can only remember that their name started with K, so I'll call them Family K. They kept fairly much to themselves and seemed to have lots of food stored in their room, as if they expected to be there for some time.

I rather maliciously thought of my father, who was likely to be engaged in battle very soon, while this young, fat Russian was just relaxing with his family, often strumming his guitar. It soon became apparent to us that K could not be trusted.

The second bedroom was occupied by a nice young mother, Jos, and her three well-behaved children. Then there was Olga, a concert pianist and her beautiful little blond, curly-headed three-year-old Willem Jan, whom she called Wanya. They lived in a tiny little room just big enough for the two of them to sleep in.

Olga was also Russian with jet black curly hair. She had beautiful hands and slender, piano-playing fingers. She would quite often drum her supple fingers on the table top as if she was playing the grand piano at a concert. She must have missed her piano very much and I deeply sympathised with her, because after Pappa, my piano was the thing I missed the most.

The bungalow had electricity, which was only used at night, and a good water supply. It had a good bathroom and a large fully-equipped kitchen with a big wood-burning stove. There was a huge pile of firewood in a tiny shed at the back of the house and there was another little storage room next to the kitchen, which was soon to be converted into a bedroom to house a Dutch woman and her young son.

We were fairly isolated in this house, which was on a hill with a large garden which sloped down to the road in the front and to a deep ravine at the back. The bungalow was not visible from the road and the ravine had a track through it which led to the village, a 10 or 15 minute walk.

Leida and I spent a lot of time in the garden and befriended a peacock which was quite tame and provided the two of us with many beautiful displays of its plumage. We also spent long periods high up in one of the tall trees on the sloping part of the garden, which afforded us a magnificent view of the majestic landscape and of the winding, silver ribbon of road we had travelled on.

We had only been there a short time when we were woken in the middle of the night. All the lights were switched on and all of a sudden everyone was standing round the large dining table. There was a very handsome man with sky-blue eyes and platinum blond hair. He was Olga's husband Willem Jan Duivene-de-Wit and he looked exhausted and very worried.

Willem Jan was high up in the Dutch airline KLM and had driven an airline bus with supplies for his wife and son to Malino in the dead of night. He had very bad news. A Japanese invasion is imminent and he was, in fact, risking his life coming to Malino. He had to return as soon as all the food supplies were stored in Olga's little room.

He said a long and tear-filled farewell to Olga and Wanya, who was the spitting image of his father, and drove away into the night. He made it back to Makassar and I believe he survived the war as a prisoner in the civilian camp at Pare Pare, about 200km up the coast from Makassar.

After Willem Jan had gone all the adults and Leida and I were sick with worry. We all felt very uneasy not knowing what was going to happen and when. Nothing is so nerve-wracking as uncertainty.

Temporarily we had a distraction as more women and children began arriving in Malino. We got a mother and her little son. They occupied the little room next to the kitchen and Mamma, Leida, Lia and I moved into the garage. They found two double bunkbeds for us and Leida and I slept in the top one and Mamma and Lia in the bottom bunk.

An Indonesian man-servant turned up one day and offered his services. Of course, he had to be paid a wage and this expense was shared by every adult. He chopped wood for the stove, cleaned the house and kept the garden tidy.

As there was only one kitchen and one stove, the women decided to take turns cooking the food. Everybody had money, so each person had to pay her share. K and his wife also had to reluctantly take turns in cooking the meals and paying for their share of the food.

Then every woman got a job. Mamma and Olga went to the market in the village every day to buy food from the natives who brought their produce there.

As there was no icebox in the house, fresh food had to be bought daily. Tante Dora and Jos got themselves a job as shop assistants. Only K and his wife did not do much.

The women had to take turns, too, to clean the bathroom and toilet. Leida and I, being teenagers, were also included in the domestic duties roster. We had to set the table, wash the dishes and do the general laundry of teatowels and tableclothes. At that time meals were quite dignified. We all sat around the large dining table, which was always nicely set with the Chinese doctor's linen tablecloth, crockery and cutlery. There were even snow-white linen serviettes – all very nice things.

To wash the dishes, water would be brought to the boil, on the wood stove because there was no water heater, in the biggest enamel pot with two handles. Extremely hot and heavy work.

Leida and I were not happy. We had never done any house chores before, as we always had Indonesian servants. We really were quite spoilt, but of course this work was nothing compared with the work we would soon be toiling at.

And I did miss Pappa, my piano and my books and school terribly. There was nothing at all to stimulate the brain. It was absolutely soul destroying and incredibly boring.

But soon the teachers from Makassar arrived in Malino. So when we were not labouring on our domestic chores, they taught us in little groups and in different locations. I was very pleased. To attend school I had to walk the single track through the ravine as all the teachers were living on the other side. But I didn't mind as it was such a lovely walk through that beautiful forest.

5. Enemy at the Door

On February 7, 1942, a Japanese fleet was approaching the southern side of Makassar and would reach the city very soon. As it was, they sailed to the south of Makassar and the Japanese soldiers rode to the city on bicycles – hundreds of them armed to the teeth – and their quiet, stealthy approach surprised the Dutch defenders of the city, many of whom were killed.

On February 8, the whole commercial district including the harbour buildings, were razed to avoid the Japanese taking possession of them. Seventy kilometres away in Malino we could see the glow of the enormous fires. We had no idea what was going on, but it was an eerie sight which filled us all with much trepidation.

Soon after the Japanese landed on Celebes, enemy planes flew over Malino, obviously on a reconnaissance mission. Then one early morning the Japanese machine-gunned Malino from the air and later dropped two light bombs. Fortunately there were no casualties. This was our first taste of aerial bombardments and it was a very frightening experience.

Apparently their target had been the shed full of cars in the centre of Malino. This shed contained the cars, minus their parts, in which the people had been transported from Makassar. Tante Dora's car was one of them.

People in Malino thought the enemy mistook the shed for an army depot. That was not to be the first time air raids were to be directed at us because of mistaken identity. We were all petrified, as were the locals, who stopped bringing their produce to the market.

The Japanese got the car parts back later when they came to Malino. They took the private cars for their own use and even shipped a large number of these cars to Japan. We didn't know it then, but the Japanese also looted our homes in Makassar, burning all photos, books and documents and shipping all the valuables to Japan, apparently promising to return them after the war. Of course they never did and up to this day we have received no compensation.

On February 23, when Leida and I were sitting in our tree high above ground, we saw a worm-shaped thing crawling along the only road between Makassar and Malino. At first we were fascinated. What could it be? It was still a long way off crawling over the windy road, moving at a snail's pace.

It was very quiet all around us, with only the birds singing and chirping. Above us the sun was smiling down on us. Malino had such a lovely climate, never too hot in the mountains and I never suffered the headaches I was to be plagued with later.

The worm kept on crawling slowly. It was like a silent movie. For a moment it would disappear round a bend in the road, then a bit later reappear.

By now Leida and I were becoming increasingly apprehensive. When the thing was close enough to be distinguished, we saw to our horror that the worm thing crawling along the road was in fact a great number of military trucks full of armed soldiers.

Leida and I slid down the tree as fast as we could and raced inside the house to tell Mamma. Her face turned deathly pale. Soon the whole house heard the news and there was a look of dread and fear on all the faces. Mamma and the other women thought of their husbands in Makassar. One thing was dreadfully clear. The Dutch had not defeated the Japanese in Makassar and we would not be returning to our quiet little lives within the three weeks promised. Despondent was probably not a word I knew as a 13-year-old, but despondent we were.

Enemy at the Door

The military trucks arrived in Malino bringing 2000 Japanese soldiers and in no time the rising sun was flying from every flagpole.

Immediately rumours began floating around about atrocities being com mitted by Japanese soldiers, including raping women and teenage girls. Mamma was very concerned about Leida and me, so she locked us up in the little woodshed to protect us from the 'rampaging Japs'.

For about a week Leida and I had to sit on the woodpile in the stuffy little shed, listening for any 'enemy visitors'. We kept absolutely quiet and so still we could almost hear our heartbeats thumping in our chests. We were only allowed to come out for meals, toilet visits and at night. That was a horrible, most frightening time, when fear obviously kept boredom at bay.

The Japs did not come to the doctor's house immediately because it was hidden from view. It was situated at the end of a very long and winding rough track of a drive which was covered with high grass and weeds. From the road the drive just looked like a neglected dead-end track.

Unfortunately, our luck ran out when our 'friend' K, the Russian, came home one morning in a car with some Japanese officers. He took them into his room, where they seemed to be having a jolly time engaged in jovial conversation while enjoying drinks, presumably supplied by K. If we hadn't already realised, we knew this man could not be trusted. We had a collaborator in our midst.

Mamma could no longer hide Leida and me now that the Japanese knew of our house among the bushes and frequently visited at all hours. At first a group of young Japanese journalists appeared with cameras. They brought flowers and biscuits for everyone. These young men were actually very polite, although they were also very alien. After they dispensed with the social duties they took the little children away, each Jap picking up a Dutch or Russian child, setting them on their shoulders. I was absolutely horrified when I saw one of them pick up little four-and-a-half year old Lia, swing her on his shoulders and disappear down the weed-covered track with the others

I cried out to Mamma, who told me that the Japanese men had assured the mothers they would return the children and they kept their promise. We never found out where they had been or what they had done, but the children were quite happy. They never cried, not even when they were carried away.

Mamma and Tante Dora had a visit from an Indonesian who had been employed by Dutch peòple in Makassar before the war. He did not have a car or a bike and most likely walked the whole 70km to Malino, risking his life to call on us. He told Mamma and Tante Dora that he had seen both Pappa and Oom Henk, who were taken prisoner. He had seen Pappa working in a field cutting the long, tough weedlike grass with a scythe. At that time both men still looked in good health so the loyal Indonesian assured the women.

Mamma and Tante Dora gave the brave man some money before he left. They could not convey their gratitude enough and they were aware the small amount of money they gave him was really insufficient for the risk he took. Many Indonesians had turned against the Dutch since the Japanese invasion, many through fear and not really getting a choice from their new masters. But this man had stayed loyal and had delivered such important and reassuring news. We never saw him again and often wondered what had happened to him. Poor Pappa and Oom Henk, what would become of them? This was now a constant worry to us all even though today's news told us they were still alive.

Suddenly our Indonesian man servant disappeared. We never found out why he had left and where he had gone to, but we discovered our beautiful peacock had been killed. The only part of the bird left were its legs and claws, which were hung above the door in the shape of a cross. Leida and I were devastated. It was such a beautiful creature and it was a wonderful sight when it spread its magnificent plumage. I found one large feather with the typical peacock pattern on it, which I kept for some time.

With our Indonesian servant gone, K was obliged to chop wood for the stove. He did it very reluctantly, lazy man that he was. We never knew what made K tick because he and his wife never talked to us and his children didn't play with the others.

(We actually met K and his family in Sydney after the war. How they got there, nobody knows but in probably the longest conversation we ever had with him, he said he would rather have gone to a prisoner of war camp "because I had a hard time". Our hearts bled for him...)

It was at times like that that I really missed my Pappa, my piano, my books and our close-knit family life. Except for the little time we had school, boredom ruled my life. Mind you, in Kampili, I often looked back at this phase of the war with a sort of melancholic yearning.

6. Rumours of my Death

Life had to go on. Everyone had chores to do and one of the jobs Leida and I had was washing the dishes.

One morning before our Indonesian servant left, it was my turn to wash the breakfast dishes and the servant had put the biggest enamel cooking pot with water on the stove and stoked the stove so I would have boiling water to do the dishes with.

As I was not very tall, I could just lift the big pot off the stove holding it with potholders on both handles. The sink was on the other side of the kitchen and higher than the stove and I had to set the pot on the edge of the sink in order to change my grip to pour the water into the basin. I didn't realise the pot was not properly balanced and the heavy pot tipped over, pouring the boiling water over my stomach and thighs. The pan clattered to the floor and I ran out of the kitchen to the garage, grabbed a towel, pulled down my very thin shorts and pants and rubbed the towel over the wet area which was very red and started to burn.

Only Leida and I were at home at the time and Leida came running. All I could do was laugh hysterically, which didn't amuse Leida at all. She ran inside to get some cream from Mamma's small leather medicine satchel.

I had always admired Leida and looked up to her. She always knew what to do and she wasn't shy like I was. I also thought she was a lot prettier than me with her big brown eyes and brown hair. My eyes are blue and at the time my hair was golden with a reddish tint.

By now I had stopped laughing. I was shivering so much my teeth were chattering. Leida smeared the cream over the scolded areas on my stomach and thighs but it made the pain worse. I was in agony.

In the meantime the others were arriving home. Mamma was deeply shocked and upset. Olga came quickly with a bottle of very good and very expensive salad oil her husband had brought her. The oil soothed the burns but did not prevent huge blisters coming up all over the scolded areas. On my thighs the blisters were as big as saucers.

I had to lie flat on my back in a bottom bunk. I could not wear any clothes except for a little top. The servant made some thin arches from bamboo which Mamma placed over me and over these arches she draped a sheet. I was lying under this white dome for several weeks suffering dreadful pain from the burns.

Although there were no painkillers or medicines in the house, Dr Goedbloed from the village across the ravine was not called. I had reason later to be thankful for this wonderful lady doctor later in the war.

When I was finally able to get up, I had to learn to walk again. The skin was very tight and I felt uncomfortable for some time. Fortunately I was young, still in good health and had a strong will to bounce back. Everybody was very supportive too and I did not have to wash the dishes again, but I did have to dry them.

In the meantime a rumour had circulated in the village that I had died of my burns. Imagine the stares of the people when they saw me walking around!

7. Showing Respect

One day we had a visit from a Japanese captain called Ino. At that stage the adults were not really scared of the Japs and we all stood on one side of the big dining table and he on the other. The K family was absent.

Ino was an ugly, short and thickset man with cropped hair, bandy legs and a bull's neck. He had what I thought was a sadistic grin on his round face and narrow menacing eyes behind thick lenses. He oozed cruel authority and had utter contempt for us.

He gave us a lecture in broken Dutch which sounded ridiculous and I felt the urge to laugh, but managed to control myself. He accused the Dutch women of being impertinent and arrogant. The victorious soldiers of the Japanese Imperial Army would teach them to be obedient. We were, in fact, at their mercy, he said.

The climax of this horrible little man's proud-as-a-peacock speech came when he announced that the war would last at least 80 years and none of us would survive. The women opposite all had a disdainful smile on their faces. One of them said flippantly: "Well, if the war lasts 80 years, you would not survive either.'

As I watched Ino's face I got really scared. The veins in his neck swelled up, his face turned crimson and I had never seen such a nasty look in a person's eyes before. I was sure he was going to hit the speaker, but he stopped short. Perhaps he thought that as he was heavily outnumbered, it was better to stop short of violence – and besides, the big table was between him and his tormentor.

After he left, we all roared with laughter and we all had great fun imitating him. There was the possibility he would return, possibly with reinforcements, but he didn't.

More women and children were arriving in Malino from the interior, northern and eastern parts of Celebes, bringing a lot more luggage than we were allowed to bring.

We had to share our already cramped quarters with some of these evacuees. We had to make room in the garage for a missionary's wife, whom we called Tante Leen, though she was a total stranger to us. She was a devout and strict Protestant who used to teach domestic chores to native girls from her husband's congregation.

In Malino she practised her teaching skills on Leida and me, as we had to do most of the domestic chores. She made us wash the floors four times, twice wet and twice dry and we loathed the job. We never had a sponge or any other handy aid to lighten this soul-destroying work. We had to get down on our knees and wash the floor with a cloth. Having to wash the floors once was bad enough, but four times was more than I could stand. We always had to do this awful job when Mamma was away buying our food at the shops and market in the village.

Fortunately for our sanity, Tante Leen was moved to more comfortable accommodation in another house. We pitied the occupants.

Money was running scarce and Mamma discovered one day that someone, and we all suspected K, had helped himself to some of the meagre cash remaining, but of course it was her word against his.

But Mamma wasn't the only one we believe he robbed. Olga was ordered to go to Makassar with the Japs and took little Wanya with her. Before she left she locked up her little room and hid the key. Nobody knew where it was.

While she was away, probably being grilled by the Kenpeitai – the Japanese equivalent of the German Gestapo – supposedly because of her husband's position with the Dutch airline KLM, someone had been stealing from her food supply. How K got into Olga's tiny room without anybody noticing is a mystery to us. We were certain none of the other women would steal from another and knew it must have been the sneaky Russian.

We all felt terribly sorry for Olga. She was away for over a week and had probably had a frightful time at the hands of her interrogators, which she was not allowed to tell anybody about. She was very quiet from then on. It must have been hard to suffer as she must have, not to be able to talk about it, and then have some food stolen.

She had a frightful row with K over the food. The two did not like each other from the start because he was a White Russian and Olga was a Red, and the dreadful slanging match in Russian made the atmosphere in the house horrible to live in. Everyone was affected by the tense atmosphere and Olga got none of the food back. Her word against his – again.

Soon afterwards, the Japanese prohibited all schooling, which was a devastating blow to Leida and me. But those marvelous women, whose names I unfortunately cannot remember, decided to carry on their teaching. In very small groups with one teacher for each group, we continued to have school in different locations all over Malino.

But after a while these clandestine lessons became too dangerous as there seemed to be more and more Japanese soldiers in the village.

The Japs ordered all books to be handed in, except bibles and cookbooks. As we could not buy most of the ingredients for recipes in the cookbooks, they had become useless.

Then it was decided that individual money supplies owned by the evacuated Dutch people from the whole village had to be handed in and held in a fund administered by a Dutchman from Makassar who had come to Malino about the same time as us. He was ordered to give each person 15 cents a day, which meant between the four of us we got the princely sum of 60 cents. Shopping was now done en masse, but as the natives were forbidden to supply us any more, food shopping was a bit of a lottery. Our diet, to be shared by the 35 inhabitants of the doctor's house, was deteriorating and consisted of corn, beans, sugar and fruit, but for how long nobody knew.

The Japanese were getting meaner by the day. They seemed to have a terrible inferiority complex, because they kept telling us we were still too arrogant and we had too much free time. We had to learn to obey and show respect for the Japanese, our conquerors. We were ordered to assemble in a field in the centre of Malino. The little children were left at home in the care of one adult. Of course this did not apply to K and his family, being friends of the Japanese.

As we stood lined up in the blazing sun opposite the Japanese army officer wearing very dark glasses, and his henchmen at his side, the little man snarled at us angrily. He would teach us to respect the Japanese and above all we had to learn to bow, not just with a nod of the head but from the waist down as far as possible. We had to bow to every Jap we met, the wee man said. So we had to rehearse bowing there and then.

I can still see us standing there. Dutch women young and old, tall and short, some with blond hair and blue eyes, others with brown hair and brown or hazel eyes or black hair and very dark eyes. Opposite this lineup of fair-skinned women stood the Japanese officer and two lower ranking Japs. We were now in their hands and at their mercy. There was nobody to defend us. They had taken everything away from us, except the miserable few things which fitted in one small suitcase. They were now in the process of taking away our dignity.

We did not have the slightest thing in common with these strange little men. They were as alien to us as we were to them but they had the power and they loved it. The officer's contempt for us was very obvious. He hated us.

At this stage the women did not take this man or his threats seriously, but they had underestimated the evil little man behind his dark glasses. He barked the order, in Japanese, to bow from the waist down.

One tall woman with very light hair and sky-blue eyes said in Dutch something along the lines of: "If you think I'm going to bow for you, you ugly bandy-legged bastard, you've got another think coming." She refused to bow. The officer in his fine uniform was obviously seething with rage that anyone, in particular a woman, and a white woman at that, would disobey him. He probably did not understand what she had said but she had refused to bow and in fact was standing up very straight.

It was a very tense moment before he gave a sign with his head to one of his henchmen who then walked over to the disobedient woman and punched her with a closed fist with all his might on the face. He face was badly damaged and quickly turned shades of black and blue.

Everyone was very shocked and upset. I was absolutely petrified and shattered at witnessing this cruel action. Then somebody down the line said softly, but loud enough for us to hear: "For God's sake, do as the man says or we'll all be beaten up."

Life was getting tougher. Radios, watches, wedding rings and anything of possible value were confiscated. Mamma was very clever. She had one ball of knitting cotton in her bag and she wound the cotton around our watches and both wedding rings. She kept this ball and it's valuable booty in her large leather handbag. She always had this bag very close to her and never let it out of her sight.

Now that Tante Leen had gone, we had to make room for two other women, Salvation Army nurses by the names of Schot and Huibregse, who had come from a hospital deep in the interior. These two women were, after Mamma and Pappa, the most wonderful people I have ever met. They were selfless, good humoured and above all, they were real samaritans. I shall never forget them. We immediately took to them and we became great friends.

At that time I had to sleep on a large wooden chest which we found in the Chinese doctor's house, which was now bursting at the seams. I had to give up my bunk and the chest was brought into the garage. On the top, a bed was made for me, which was not at all comfortable. It was hard and too short, so I could not stretch my legs out. But it had to do. At least I still had a bed.

8. Illness and Death

I fell violently ill in the middle of the night soon after the bowing episode and thought I was going to die. I vomited all night and had the most excruciating, stabbing pain in my abdomen – someone was knifing me in the stomach. I also had a splitting headache, the sort that feels as if your head is ready to burst.

Mamma was beside herself with worry. There was no telephone and the only doctor, Dr Goedbloed, lived in the village across the valley. It was pitch-dark and far too dangerous to walk through the forested ravine to fetch her.

Finally, after a terrifying night not only for me but also for Mamma and the other people living in the garage, the attack wore off. Our new 'room-mates', the Salvation Army nurses, were convinced I had suffered an attack of appendicitis.

I was greatly comforted by the two dedicated nurses. One of them, whom we called 'Schotje' (her surname was Schot) assured me that in the case of an emergency she could operate on me and remove the offending appendix. She came from the heartland of Celebes, a very primitive region where there were neither hospital nor proper medical facilities, so one had to make do.

As it happened, and lucky for me, there was no other attack at that time, but I was weak and suffered headaches and a constant niggling pain in my stomach. I felt really wretched.

At that time there were a lot of burglaries going on. The locals, who could not work or sell their produce, were reduced to poverty. There were native guards but they could not be everywhere at night.

Our garage dormitory had no lock. Mamma had invented an ingenious burglary detection system by hanging a petrol tin containing some glass marbles on the inside of the garage door by a small window.

One night I woke up with a start. There was a bit of faint light coming in through the little garage door window and the marbles were rattling inside the petrol tin. Then I saw a hand through the broken glass of the little window reaching out to open the door. I was very frightened but I managed to wake Mamma and put my finger against her lips to indicate to her to be silent while I pointed to the door.

Mamma got up quickly and quietly and picked up the wooden stick she kept under her pillow, softly walked to the door with the still groping hand trying to find the latch and hit it hard. A kind of groan was heard on the outside and the hand disappeared immediately along with the would-be thief whose hand it was.

After that incident we did not sleep soundly again. We were never sure of anything at that time. We were very vulnerable and defenceless. The little window, the only natural light in the garage, was lost forever as there was no way it could be fixed.

Some time later we lost our home away from home because the Japanese wanted the doctor's house for themselves. We had to move out and went to other houses across the ravine whether there was room or not. The occupants of the doctor's house, all of whom with the exception of K and his family we counted as friends, were separated.

Our new house was already full, so we got the garage again. This was even smaller than the other one and we were very cramped. The Japanese were taking other houses as well, so more and more people needed accommodation, with fewer houses available.

The rains came, making things extremely difficult for us. We had to cope with wet wood, wet clothes and illness. Having to stay indoors with so many people in cramped circumstances was nerve-wracking. We had absolutely no privacy at all.

One young boy of nine was a diabetic. His insulin supply had been used and no more was available. He fell seriously ill and died. His poor mother was devastated and inconsolable and his death had a profound effect on all of us living in that house.

And then Mrs Schiphorst, the mother of my best friend after the war in Holland, Lily, suddenly died and was buried in Malino. Lily and her younger sister and brother were cared for from then on by a young unmarried woman friend of the family.

From this sad and gloomy period came even harsher orders from the Japanese. They ordered the native administration to undertake a book hunt and they uncovered numerous caches of books which had escaped previous confiscations. Bibles, hymn books and the by now totally useless cookbooks were spared.

The spiteful Japanese believed all the women did was cook their own meals and sleep. They reckoned the women were still too jolly and had too much leisure time, so reading books was absolutely out of the question.

On top of that there were now persistent rumours that we were going to be moved to another location. According to the rumours, the Japanese thought Malino, with its lovely climate, was far too good for us and we did not deserve to live there. And yes, the rumours soon became reality and we had to leave Malino.

9. Leaving Malino

In the beginning of May 1943, we were told to prepare for departure to an unknown destination. We had been in Malino for 16 months and experienced a lot. I, as a 14-year-old, had experienced far more than I would have wanted but there were so many in the same boat as me. Children were growing up very fast out of the need to survive and this became even more of a necessity in the two-and-a-half years before our nightmare at Kampili ended.

All the ex-pat women and children in Malino, who numbered about 1300, were 'trucked out' in three days. We were included in the last group to leave. The trucks were high army lorries which were roofless and without seats. We were not allowed to bring mattresses, so Mamma took some pillows to sit on. She also took some other articles from the house which we could pack in our one suitcase, such as a cast iron rice cooker and a little pot.

We had very little left of the things which Mamma had packed in the suitcase all that time ago in Makassar when we had to pack and be evacuated in a hurry, so Mamma also crammed in some things we would certainly need in our new accommodation, such as a sheet or two and a couple of towels.

There was a ginger tom cat at the house, which was cared for by everyone. As there would be only Japanese left, who almost certainly would not have been bothered to look after a cat, Leida and I decided to take him with us. We fed him well and gave him a bit of an alcoholic drink made of eggs, sugar and some alcohol, which was then beaten till it was properly mixed and fluffy. This made the cat, whom we called Peter, sleepy.

The Japs loaded our meagre luggage onto the truck and decided what could be taken. Anything that failed to pass the Japanese muster was just tossed away like rubbish. When the Japs had finished loading what luggage they deemed enough for us, they ordered us to climb aboard our 'luxury' form of transport. Fortunately the Japs did not see the cat.

The Japanese spoke very little of the native language and no Dutch or English at all. We did not understand Japanese, so communication was very limited and difficult. The Japs just barked at us and we were supposed to understand them.

The truck was old and very uncomfortable and it was obvious it had not been serviced for some time. We had to sit on the floor of the open truck in the blazing sun while the Japanese driver and his mate sat in the cabin.

Malino had a lovely climate, situated as it is high up in the mountains. It was never very hot there, but now we were travelling away from the cool fresh air. The more we descended, the hotter it became and we started to sweat in temperatures in the high 20s or 30s with high humidity.

In the unbearable heat bumping along that road we wondered where they were taking us and what they were going to do with us. We could not understand why we had to leave Malino. There were so many things we couldn't understand. We were just ordered to do things.

The sun continued to beat down mercilessly and we were tossed about like rubber balls. Poor Mamma was sick. She had a small tin at hand that had once, in the good old days of peace, contained Haagse Hopjes – small sweets – and she soon filled that up.

I was still quite weak after the appendicitis attack and I felt a splitting headache coming on. At that time I suffered a lot from these head-splitters. Peter the cat was sleeping peacefully in my shadow – the only thing in the back of that lorry which wasn't suffering.

Suddenly the truck gave up. It had broken down and the Japs took their time to fix it, while we just sat there baking and soaking with sweat. The Japanese always snapped at us and were the most unfriendly and strange people I had ever known. They carried guns and bayonets as if they feared we would try to escape. Goodness me, where could we go? Surely they did not think we would attack them. But I was rather scared.

Not knowing where we were going, Mamma being sick, and myself not in the best of health either. We had no idea where Pappa was, or if he was still alive. All this worried me a great deal. Why did we have to suffer all this? Why were these strange little armed men allowed to treat us in this manner? In my 14-year-old's mind, it just did not make any sense.

Sometimes we saw natives standing by the roadside staring at us. They looked at us in bewilderment. Seeing European women and their children being carted off in such an unceremonious way was beyond them.

10. Kampili

After hours of bouncing up and down, and more dead than alive, we reached our destination. We drove along a canal of brown, muddy water, over a bridge spanning the canal and through a large gate onto a driveway with grass fields on either side leading to a main building.

On the right hand side of the main building stood a row of tiny houses, while on our left we saw two large complexes, each consisting of six long bamboo barracks with walls constructed of wicker-work bamboo and roofs made of overlapping palm leaves.

We drove up the driveway and came to a halt in front of the main brick building. We were just about tossed off the truck and fell into very high, tough grass. I almost disappeared into the grass but little Lia was totally swallowed up by it. I could just see over the top, standing on tiptoe. There had not been any rain for some time. The tough grass was yellow and the whole place was hot and dry.

We learnt that originally Kampili had been a sanitorium for tuberculosis sufferers. The row of little houses we had seen as we drove in were occupied by people who had come from the offshore island of Ambon, where they had been bombed out of their camp.

Kampili was about 30km south of Makassar and was the most primitive, dreary and depressing place. There was a barbed wire fence all round the compound but we did not get the chance to look around.

Some Japanese soldiers came and rudely herded us in one direction. I grabbed Peter, who was still a bit groggy and my little suitcase, Leida took Lia by the hand and Mamma picked up the big suitcase containing our entire possessions and put the bulging leather handbag on her arm. This bag went wherever Mamma went.

The Japanese carried guns and to me they looked menacing. We were separated from the people on our truck and ordered to walk to a long bamboo barrack, the last one of complex B which consisted of barracks seven to 12. When we arrived at the front opening of barrack 12 the Japs went away.

Our barrack consisted of a frame made of whole bamboo stalks tied together with strips of bamboo bark. This bamboo proved to be the ideal nesting place for rats – huge ones.

Through the front opening we saw bare bamboo bunks, top and bottom ones lining both walls of the barrack. There was a little bamboo ladder at the foot of each top bunk to climb up. There were doors at regular distances on both sides of the long barrack. The doors and walls were made of thin wicker-work type bamboo and the doors were tied to the walls on one side with bark. The roof was the overlapping palm leaves, while the floor was just reddish coloured earth. Between the bunks there were tiny cubicles and absolutely nothing else.

There were 100 bunks to each barrack and mercifully every person was entitled to one, so once inside we set about finding two sets of bunks together for our family. We were not the first people in the barrack as earlier Malino arrivals already occupied most of the bunks.

Near the front of the barrack on our right we saw a woman sitting on a bottom bunk sobbing loudly. Her three little daughters, all redheads like mum, stood in front of her, also crying, the tears rolling down their little freckled faces. Mamma resolutely walked up to the foursome, with a stern face, said to the woman: "Stop your crying immediately. This isn't going to help you or your girls. We are all in the same dreadful circumstances. We just have to get used to it."

The woman, Mrs de Kloe, snivelled for a while, dried her eyes and wiped the pretty little faces of her cute daughters. Then she got up to settle down in the tiny cubicle between their two sets of bunks. Later on we got to know her quite well and she turned out to be a very nice and helpful person.

Mamma, Leida, Lia and I did not cry as it was no use really. Mamma found us a tiny cubicle, flanked on both sides by a top and bottom bunk about halfway down the barrack on the left-hand side. We were in the last barrack of complex B, which meant we had no neighbours on our side, which was I suppose, a bit of a bonus.

We looked out on a small grass area and in the corner near us, inside the barbed wire fence, was a beautiful, majestic tree which was also a captive in our camp. It spread its magnificent foliage out like a large umbrella.

Beyond the barbed wire were bare, dried out sawahs or paddy fields. Nobody had tilled these fields for a long time. Across the dirty canal on the opposite side of the road we could see some bush. It was so hot the air was hazy and heat quivered above the naked land while the sun continued beating down. It was really unbearably hot, even inside the barrack. There was no sign of rain in the blue, cloudless sky.

Here we were completely cut off from the rest of the world where war raged, even from a native village not far away. We were separated from the world by a barbed wire fence so there was no way we could communicate with anybody outside the fence. How the war was going, who was winning and when will it end? Impossible questions with no answers.

Having so long been captives of the Japanese at a distance and with relative freedom, we were now in a compound under lock, key and barbed wire. Real prisoners.

We had no power, sewerage, reticulated water, radio, telephone or the privacy of a bathroom. There was nothing but those bare barracks. It was horrible but there was nothing anybody could do about it. This hot, simmering nothingness was now our home.

And there was nothing to do. In the beginning, life in the camp was rather chaotic but soon the women with leadership talents organised the management of the daily camp routine, although they always had to bear in mind they had to obey the camp commandant Tadasji Yamaji's orders.

Soon, all the people who were able to work were put in different groups and were assigned jobs.

But before that, Leida and I were bored stiff. We kicked our heels and generally felt miserable with no books to read, pianos to play, or songs to sing. But one day soon after we arrived we came across something to keep us occupied.

Around barrack number 12 there was lots of builders' rubble lying around. The builders had not quite finished building the camp and neither had they tidied up. While looking at all the rubble, particularly pieces of bamboo, Leida and I had the brilliant idea of making our own domino game. It would give us something to do to kill the boring hours and be a welcome distraction and we were quite excited at thinking of such a fun game.

We searched the rubble for small bits of bamboo, which were plentiful, and then we cut them into smaller rectangular pieces and divided them into two equal spaces like a domino tablet. We also marked on each domino the spots which we would burn into the bamboo.

We were lucky enough to find a small shard of white glass and painstakingly we held the little piece of glass above the bamboo tablets, caught the sun and burnt little dots. We thought we were very clever.

Leida and I took turns at burning the dots and patiently we held the glass above half-space after half-space of our domino set, which was often quite difficult because the sun was so hot. Lack of attention would mean the dots would be too big and there wouldn't be enough room on the tablet for the required number of dots. Six dots was very hard to do.

For our game we had to make 28 such pieces and we also made a neat little dice, which was a difficult proposition because the sides of the dice were of course much smaller than the tablets of our dominoes, so burning six dots was an even more difficult proposition.

When we were finished, we had produced a real work of art. We had really enjoyed making the dominoes but that was nothing to the enjoyment of playing it. We played for hour after hour and even managed to teach five-year-old Lia how to play.

But when the Japs ordered us to work, our domino game, which had given us so much pleasure, was soon forgotten. After that we used to dream of being bored enough to play dominoes, but that was a forlorn dream because we were always so tired. And we fell ill, Leida with malaria and me with appendicitis.

Sadly our much treasured domino game was destroyed in the fire on July 17, 1945.

11. Acclimatisation

Our first meal in Kampili was better than we were used to in Malino – rice, meat and vegetables. Our dining room was a long narrow bamboo structure running across the whole front of the six barracks of complex B. We sat on hard backless bamboo benches.

Each barrack was connected to the dining room by an open walkway which consisted of a roof of palm leaves set on bamboo poles. This flimsy dining room had no walls and there were rough, primitive bamboo tables in the middle and long benches on either side. The Ritz it was not.

Our latrines were situated at the back of the barracks and consisted of a hole in the ground with a little raised step to place your feet. The squatting toilets had no flush and the holes ran into some sewer pits behind the latrines. There was a whole row of these primitive lavatories along the back of the six barracks and they were joined by a short walkway. The walls and roofs of the 'loos' were the same as everything else, bamboo and palm leaves. Each toilet had a flimsy door which would soon fall apart, not being able to cope with the intensive use. We had no toilet paper, nor water and of course no soap. To wash our hands we had to go to our own little place in the barrack.

We kept some water on the bamboo bench which ran along the outside of our barrack. This bench was like a drip rack and we placed our dishes on it after washing up.

Later on we were able to grow a kind of succulent plant underneath this bench. The waste was used for irrigating our precious vegetables, the leaves of which were juicy, if a bit sour. They were rich in vitamin C, which as time went on and the diet deteriorated, was a much-needed item of sustenance.

That first day we were very hot and tired from the long truck journey. We longed to have a bath, or at least a wash. There was no water near our barrack, so Leida and I set out to find some place where we could at least freshen up. It was late afternoon and the sun was beginning to slide down in the west, but it was still very hot. A lot of people, armed soldiers included, were walking around the compound.

Leida and I did find a well quite a distance from our barrack, standing in the middle of nowhere, which did not seem to belong to any building. There were no walls around the well, only a narrow concrete strip to stand on. There was no pump, so to get water we had to use a tin on a long rope, of which there was only one by that well. There were already several women and children waiting, so we had to wait our turn.

There had apparently been very little rain, so we found that there was very little water in the well and the tin had to go down an awfully long way before it reached some water to scoop up. Bathing was a very slow process but we were very grateful for the little bit of water we could haul up from the depths of that well.

Japs were walking around everywhere and we felt very uncomfortable. If one of these strange foreign little characters came close to the well where Leida and I stood naked, we just squatted behind the well wall and crept around the wall on all fours to avoid being seen. Most degrading, but that's what it took to get a bath that night.

We finished our wash as it grew dark and felt greatly relieved when we could return 'home' to barrack 12. By then it was completely dark and we had some difficulty finding our way back to our barrack. The only lights were a few dim oil lamps in the barrack. In the meantime, Mamma and Lia had also had a bath at another well.

The next morning we discovered we had mud caked on our bodies and our towels were filthy. What we thought to be clean water was in fact muddy water we had hauled up from the bottom of that well. There was no water to wash our clothes, either, so it was a hopeless situation.

Later on, wells were dug in between the barracks by natives with whom we were forbidden to communicate. They put a concrete floor down around the wells and built flimsy bamboo walls around with a roof of palm leaves. These wonderful constructions were to be our bathrooms. On either side was built a door because the well/bathroom had to be shared between barracks, which was bad luck for us in barrack 12. As we were the last barrack in the complex, the 100 or so in our room had to share with half of barrack 11 – 150 sharing the spartan facility – whereas the other half of barrack 11 had to share the bathroom between it and barrack 10 with only half of that room – about 100 people – and so on. We got the rough end of the stick, although we did have the compensation of that beautiful, big green tree and no neighbours at our end of the barrack.

There were also a number of boys in their early teens living in the camp who also had to use the bathrooms. This often caused great embarrassment. One knew when this happened as loud yells would penetrate the thin bathroom walls and the next minute a red-faced boy would fly out of the door. To avoid this, certain times were set aside for women and their children, adults and boys.

We also had to wash our clothes by the well in the bathroom. There was only one tin on a long rope, so everybody had to take turns. After a while the rope would wear out and break due to the constant use. So the tin would plunge to the bottom of the well and had to be retrieved by some hardy soul. There was only one bamboo ladder in the whole camp for this purpose, so a broken rope would often cause a lengthy delay while the ladder was found and the two joints of rope were tied back together.

Like everything, we got used to the privations of our situation, but I often think of those young mothers with babies and very young children having to cope with these extremely difficult and stressful conditions.

12. The Central Kitchen

It was far from easy cooking meals for so many people with the meagre supplies given to the people working in the kitchen. The head of the central kitchen was Mrs den Hond, a very hard working and courageous woman, who was also a great organiser.

A group of women on roster duty cooked the food in large oil drums over wood fires. While standing on some bricks or a little stool, they stirred the substances cooking in the drums with huge wooden ladles. This was very hot and tiring work but they tried their utmost to give us one hot meal a day.

There were other women engaged in cleaning vegetables and others to clean out the drums. That cleaning job was heavy and tiring work as those drums were cumbersome and heavy.

Our staple diet was white rice. For breakfast we ate rice porridge cooked in water with a tiny bit of sugar, if available. The main meal consisted of boiled rice with a watery substance in which floated kangkung leaves, which is a bitter-tasting spinach, and a few tiny pieces of meat. Three square meals were a distant memory and as a result of this diet we were often very hungry.

Once a week, if we were lucky, we were given a tiny ration of ground coffee, tea and white sugar. These tiny rations had to last at least a week, so tea leaves were saved and used over and over again, as was the ground coffee, until both beverages bore little resemblance to the original.

On a very rare occasion we were given a banana and on rarer occasions, some peanuts. The bananas were often rotten, but we ate them with relish. Once a year we were given an egg, which could also be rotten. If you got a bad egg it was bad luck, as they couldn't be replaced and it was too risky to eat a rotten egg. A bad egg recipient missed out and it was a long time between eggs.

Water for the kitchen had to be pumped out of the only well with a pump and was near the kitchen. A little group of women took turns manning the pump to fill the kitchen drums and this was very tiring work. A lot of water was needed for the kitchen, therefore the pump group had to take turns and could only pump for a short time before being relieved.

The availability of water was a constant worry. The water had to be boiled for drinking, which was done in the central kitchen.

One of the camp characters was Lily Gravelotte, who used to walk through the barracks announcing like the town crier that water for coffee or tea could be fetched from the central kitchen. Lily would make it sound rather like a song, raising or dropping some letters, in particular the a and o sounds and at the same time holding them in her particular pitch.

Lily really brought a ray of sunshine to our dismal existence, even if it was only for a short while. While she was walking and singing through our barrack, a long line of people carrying a variety of receptacles would then head for the kitchen. We actually looked forward to this daily interlude and we all liked Lily. She was good company, helpful and witty, and had a son in his early teens.

We had very little crockery or cutlery, just a few tins plates and a few forks and spoons. Leida and I used to drink from an old Camel cigarette tin.

We shared out food with Peter the tom, who always slept at the end of my bunk, which was on the top. During the night he would be out but as soon as it became daylight he would be back, purring loudly. Peter gave us a lot of pleasure.

13. The Boss

The camp commandant, Tadasji Yamaji, really was the boss and woe betide anybody who forgot it. He was a short, thick-set, bandy-legged man of about 24 but looked much older. He wore spectacles with very thick lenses and he had small, beady black eyes.

Later on we heard that he came from the civilian men's camp at Pare Pare where he had almost beaten two Dutch priests to death. He was a brute and a bully and worst of all, extremely unpredictable. During our time he beat up women and teenage boys and girls with a thick stick he always carried, or he slapped them on the face or boxed their ears. He was very good at that.

We used to call the commandant Bok'eh among ourselves. We're not sure where the nickname came from or from where it originates but it was certainly not a term of endearment. It is derived from one of the Indonesian dialects and basically it means something simple. And Bok'eh was simple alright – simply a pig and a bully.

I was very frightened of him and didn't trust him as far as I could see him. Whenever we met him or any other Jap we had to bow a deep bow from the waist down and we had to say to him and others 'Tuan', (sir) if we were spoken to. Fancy calling a brute who beat up women and girls sir.

Bok'eh had an assistant, a very young little Japanese soldier who was also beaten up for various reasons by the unpredictable monster. We called this little man Daantje (little Dan). He was a harmless little man who was really still a boy and we pitied him. As much as we loathed the Japs, we felt very sorry for Daantje.

The first sign of Bok'eh's brutality came when he discovered a smuggling ring operated by the native police guards which were used early on in our stay. Smuggling through the barbed wire became a very busy activity and handy foodstuffs like eggs, fruit and vegetables and sweets were bartered for through the wire.

We didn't know about this activity, so we couldn't take advantage of getting a little bit of luxury but we got to hear of it when the smugglers were discovered. They were not careful enough and some were caught in the act. One of the police guards who was involved with the smuggling was dragged in front of Bok'eh's house and, witnessed by many horrified onlookers, was beaten close to death by the brute Bok'eh wielding his stick, then flung out of the compound.

From then on nobody was allowed near the barbed wire fence and anyone who dared to disobey orders would be beaten up, no questions asked.

The prisoners had two leaders, Mrs Joustra for the Malino refugees and Mrs Valderpoort for the Ambon group. Each of the 12 barracks had leaders as well and they frequently held meetings.

Bok'eh appointed a woman, Mrs C. Voskuil, who had to inform the leaders of every order he gave. She also had to run and fetch any person Bok'eh wanted to see and as he gave many fetching orders and was very impatient, the poor woman was constantly on the run.

We also had two female doctors, Dr Goedbloed from Malino and Dr Feenstra. Then there was Dr Marseille, who was a bacteriologist who had been given the job of supervising hygiene, including looking after the latrines, digging sewer pits and taking care of fly eradication. It was the worst possible job and the poor man was often in the dog box and threatened with a thrashing from Bok'eh .

Besides Dr Marseille there were two other men in the camp, Mr Spreeuwenberg, a Protestant minister who was the camp carpenter and Father

Beltjens, a Catholic priest, who was the camp butcher.

At first Father Beltjens had a teenage boy as his assistant. However, the boy became ill with amoebic dysentery and although he was close to death, survived, but did not work in the butchery again. His place was taken by Lies Rooyards, who, with her two children Marian, about four or five and Wietse, a toddler of two or three, lived opposite us in barrack 12.

Lies was a very attractive woman with black wavy hair with a grey streak here and there which gave her a distinguished look. She had blue eyes and an olive complexion and had a very pleasant nature. She was patient and quiet and I liked and admired her very much.

The priest had to slaughter whatever beast was brought into the camp by natives. Usually it was one very thin buffalo no bigger than a donkey. In the beginning we would get meat every day but the meat of an emaciated little buffalo did not go far amongst 1600-1700 people. Later on we had to have meatless days, as the daily deliveries dried up.

14. Daily Life

Living in the bamboo barrack 12 was not particularly easy. Each barrack had four coconut oil lamps and we got a little bit of oil for some little individual lamps. Our lamp was simply a tiny wick floating in a bit of the oil in a small tin but it was a luxury while it lasted, which wasn't very long. Soon there was no oil for our own lamps and we had to make do with the four main ones.

The most scary part was having to go to the loo in the middle of the night. Mamma decided to use the cast iron cooker as a chamber pot as it had no more use as a cooker. At night she set it on the dirt floor in the middle of our cubicle and after use we always had to put the lid on.

In the wall by our top bunks, Leida and I cut three sides of a small square. The top was left uncut, so it formed a flap which we pushed open and held with a small stick during the day to get some air in. On the inside we fixed a piece of string to the bottom end of the flap so we could close our little window at night. We were proud of our little piece of ingenuity and in no time these little windows appeared in the walls of all the barracks.

Lying in my bunk on my stomach I would gaze through my little window and look longingly at the open space and the beautiful living tree and it would almost make me weep. I was a prisoner held in a camp behind barbed wire although I had not done anything wrong. I often wondered if we would ever be going beyond that barbed wire fence again. Would we ever live in a house again with all the facilities and sleep in a proper bed again with mattress, pillow, sheets – and a mosquito net? Would we ever eat good food again? Would we ever wear nice clothes and shoes again? So many tough questions for a 15-year-old.

We were told in no uncertain terms by the Japanese that we had to work for our living. Idleness would not be tolerated. All the teenage girls were grouped according to age and each group had an adult supervisor. We were each given a patjol, or Indonesian spade, and told we would be working on the land.

Before marching off to the dried-out sawahs (paddy fields) outside the camp with the patjol resting on our shoulder much like a rifle, we had to line up for roll call in front of the main building where Bok'eh lived and had his office. This had to be done twice a day – in the morning and after lunch.

On the land we had to hack at the hardened, infertile soil barefooted in the blazing, tropical sun with virtually no protection. Some had hats but I didn't and needed one to protect my fair skin. It was hard work that the majority of us had never had to do before and for me it was an almost impossible task as I had a niggling pain in my stomach.

That pain was a forerunner to my appendix playing up again and I had to give up work. I suffered intolerably, with excruciating pain my constant companion. There were no painkillers and sometimes I wished I could die. They put an icepack on my stomach which made it feel as if it would explode. I was in a really bad way.

We had no contact with Schotje or the other Salvation Army nurse, nor did we see any of the other housemates from Malino as they were in complex A, barrack numbers one to six.

A very kind person gave me an old deck chair so I could sit outside sometimes. But mostly I was lying in one of the bottom bunks. We had each been given a thin mat to sleep on, because we had been prohibited from bringing mattresses from Malino, and we had a few pillows, which at least gave me some comfort, although my errant appendix continued to give me no end of agony.

More people arrived from the outer islands of the archipelago and the bacteriologist, Dr Marseille, used to escort these new arrivals around the camp. He always stopped by my bunk and explained the reason I was lying there. The people looked down at me with faces full of pity. I felt as if I was on display like an animal in the zoo.

Kampili housed ex-pats from all over Celebes and it was obvious that Japanese occupying other areas of the island were more lenient than our lot that came to Malino. People from other areas had been able to bring trunks full of clothes, tinned food and bed linen. Soon people hung sheets or anything suitable between their bunks and those of their neighbours to get some privacy. We had an outside door on one side but on the other our neighbours, Mrs van Gogh and her two children, had hung a sheet between us.

One could only hang something between the bottom bunks and when lying on the top bed, mostly occupied by young people and children, you could see right through the barrack. We all slept in the clothes we wore during the day as we had no pyjamas or nighties.

Having to work hard in that hot climate and naturally sweating a lot meant we had to wash our clothes daily. But our underwear soon began to show signs of wear and tear and while Mamma and Leida were very clever dressmakers, they were soon only fit for rags.

From a sheet we had managed to pinch from the Chinese doctor's house in Malino, Mamma and Leida, who both ended up working in the sewing room making the Japanese uniforms, managed to fit in time to sew some underpants and bras for the three of us. They were so clever. While the majority of women had to make do with what they had – or do without – we had some brand new knickers and bras, even if they weren't exactly the latest in fashion.

15. The Appendectomy

I was surprised to find I was not the only one suffering the agonies of appendicitis in the camp. Dr Goedbloed pleaded with Bok'eh to request his superiors in Makassar to make it possible for we unfortunates to have an operation. She did manage to persuade him and he managed to convince his bosses of the urgent need to operate.

One day a short time later, we were told to report to one of the tiny houses where the Ambon refugees lived. This little brick building consisted of two small rooms and a bathroom and toilet and was converted into a hospital ward.

There were four of us needing the operation, two to each room. One was a young married woman, whose name I can't remember, and three teenage girls, Margriet, Miep and me.

I had no idea what this operation was like and I didn't care. I had never been ill before and had certainly never been to hospital, let alone had to undergo an operation, but I was constantly in so much pain that I almost looked forward to it. We had good beds and marvellous Dutch nurses looking after us.

The night before the operation we were given a spoonful of castor oil to clean us out. The other three were running to the toilet all night but not me, possibly because I had been unable to eat much for some time. They decided to leave me till last in the hope that the castor oil would do its job and flush me out at the 11th hour. It didn't.

The following morning after we had spent a restless and nervous night, they prepared us. It left me with a very strange feeling of nervousness mixed with excitement that my pain would soon be no more. Then they came and took the married woman away. We were assured that we would get a general anaesthetic and that we would not feel a thing. How naive can you get?

The room, called the polyclinic, had been converted into an operating theatre and while they operated on the woman the second patient, Miep, had to sit on the little porch by the operating room.

When the young woman was carried back on a bamboo stretcher, she was fully conscious. They had only given her a local anaesthetic. I was immediately feeling very scared and poor Miep and Margriet turned white as ghosts. But the courageous lady told us not to worry because really, she hadn't felt a thing. What a brave heroine she was. She must have been in great pain but she managed to hide it from us.

Miep was a girl the same age as me and she shared the little room at the back with me. Before she was brought back, Margriet had gone to wait her turn on the little porch.

When Miep was carried back on the stretcher she was the colour of the white sheet covering her. She didn't say a word and I didn't dare talk to her.

Then came my turn. I was escorted to the little porch and told to sit down on the rickety rattan chair just outside the waiting room until it was my turn to go under the knife. Dr Marseille, the bacteriologist was with me and the door and the window of the operating room were wide open and covered with mosquito netting against the flies.

It was another boiling hot day with the sun blazing away right above us. Inside the room Margriet was obviously in agony because she was screaming her head off. I became very nervous and started biting my nails, something I had never done before.

Dr Marseille was told to give me an injection and he jabbed a blunt needle into my right thigh, presumably to relax me but all it did was give me a very painful leg.

After what seemed like an eternity, a still wailing Margriet was carried out on a stretcher. Now for me. I was scared stiff now that it was really going to happen.

I had to walk into the room and I was limping from the injection Dr Marseille had given me. I was aware of a crude sterilising apparatus rather like an old-fashioned charcoal barbecue near the bed with all the operating instruments lying being cleaned by the coals. The commandant Bok'eh suddenly appeared and followed me in, walked to one corner and stood there during the whole operation.

I was told to take off my brunchcoat and then hop onto the rough wooden operating table. The Japanese surgeon and another Asian person were standing by the table. I was horribly embarrassed as I was wearing only a little cotton top which reached only my waist. To be virtually naked in front of those men and Bok'eh was horrible. It would have been bad enough for any woman but for a 15-year-old it was the stuff of nightmares.

Fortunately Dr Goedbloed was there too. Her friendly female face was something of a comfort. I had to lie down on the hard table, which was covered with a white sheet. They tied me down and covered my face with a thick towel. I asked Dr Goedbloed if the towel could be removed because it made me feel like I was about to suffocate. A short conversation in English followed between the doctor and the Japanese surgeon and the towel was replaced by a piece of gauze.

The surgeon was quite tall for a Japanese and I heard later he was a Korean and had studied in the United States. He spoke fluent English but I was not allowed to talk to him. He did not say a word to me either.

A sheet was arranged over me leaving the operating spot open. Then a needle was poked into my abdomen and that was excruciatingly painful. But that was nothing compared with the agony that followed. The injection did not seem to numb me at all.

The operation was sheer torture. No wonder Margriet had screamed so much. I was determined not to utter a sound. Dr Goedbloed was sitting on my right and took my hand saying I could squeeze her hand if it hurt. I probably did just that because I was in terrible pain as the surgeon's knife cut me open.

Through the gauze I watched the immobile oriental face of the surgeon and it was like a mask with sweat dripping off it. The surgeon requested in Japanese the instruments he needed and the other man handed them to him.

Under the sheet and the gauze I was in agony but I could not move or do anything. However, I certainly was not going to scream. It felt as if my tummy was being all cut up in pieces and on top of that misery was that oppressive, suffocating heat.

Just as I thought I could not stand it any longer, the soft friendly voice of the doctor at my right said: "Look Gerda, that's the offensive thing." She pointed to the surgeon, who held the most revolting looking thing, dangling from an instrument, right above my face. I nearly fainted. Then there was the sound of 'plop' as the thing was dropped into a container out of my sight

I felt the stitching. Every time the needle was stuck into my body I felt a sharp, stabbing pain. When that extra bit of torture was finished, they put a heavy object on top of the stitches, which was in fact a bag filled with white sand. To finish the job, a wide, white cotton band, called a gurita, was wrapped around me as tightly as possible to hold the bag with sand into place. I was in great pain and now I felt horrible discomfort from the restriction of the gurita.

Then Bok'eh left. He had not said a word.

I was placed on the stretcher and covered with a thick woollen blanket. Four people, each holding one corner, carried me back to the little ward. The stretcher was sloping to one side because the bearers were of different height and I was petrified that I would roll off. I clung to one side, which caused excruciating pain in my abdomen. The sun was beating down and it was unbearably hot under that blanket but I did not complain. Fortunately it was only a short distance from that little room of torture to the tiny ward.

The Dutch nurses were really lovely and dedicated. They always tried to cheer us up. One nurse told us jokes but laughing was a painful exercise. Another nurse, a little dark haired woman, had a hernia the size of a duck's egg and by stretching her thin smock over the shape we could see the size of it. She went under the surgeon's knife sometime later.

The other three appendectomy victims seemed to be recovering well but I wasn't. I became very ill and my temperature rose to a dangerous level. I couldn't eat and I was constantly in great pain. Bok'eh came every day to see how we were doing and he asked Dr Goedbloed why I was not improving. She told him I urgently needed medicine.

One kind person gave me some butter in which some liver was fried for me but I could not eat it. Nor could I eat the tinned fruit another donor gave me, so the other patients got the treats.

The fever would not go down and everybody was worried about me. Poor Mamma. It must have been terrible for her to see me suffering like that and at that time she was not feeling very well either.

Bok'eh came again and demanded to know what the matter was with me and why I was so very ill. The good Dr Goedbloed stressed again that I needed medicines most urgently, so the next time the commandant came he had some white pills which he had apparently travelled to Makassar to get.

After taking these pills regularly I slowly started to pick up. Because I had become very weak and thin they brought me to the little hospital. The surgeon came back after about two weeks and he came to see me.

I heard the doctor and the surgeon talking, in English, about an abscess. I was not allowed to speak to the surgeon.

16. Mamma's Illness

I wasn't allowed to do any work for a while. Sister Makaria, head of the small women's hospital, ordered that I be given a daily portion of rice cooked in milk to get my strength back. There were a few dairy cows in the camp grazing on a small grassed area which was called 'the meadow'. Milk was only for very sick people but I was very grateful to that beautiful nun.

When I was nearly back to the stage that I could work again, Bok'eh decided to scare the daylights out of me. He would sneak up and blurt out: "Moesti potong lagi." He was learning the native language and that meant I had to be "cut" again, or operated on a second time.

I was petrified in my naivety. Suppose he was right? After all, he was there when they had operated on me. I went to Dr Goedbloed, who assured me that nothing was further from the truth. Bok'eh liked to scare people, she said, and in my case he had certainly succeeded.

Lia was born asthmatic and she suffered a lot in that camp. When she had an attack her little thin face would turn purple and it was terrible seeing our little sister gasping for breath and almost suffocating. At first Mamma had some tablets but the supply was soon exhausted and she could not get any more, so little Lia continued to suffer.

Mamma used to do the hospital laundry, all by hand in a wooden tub. It was very hard manual work and she would be standing at the old tub for hours with her hands and arms in the suds. Day in and day out she toiled and at the end of each day she was exhausted. Her beautiful fine hands which had made many magnificent things in fine embroidery, crochet and knitting, were red and rough.

And after a time Mamma fell very ill with dysentery, the scourge of the camp, basically caused by the lack of clean water. Its symptoms are diarrhoea with blood, fever, stomach cramps and not being able to keep anything down. It was very contagious. The disease was often fatal and killed 10 people at Kampili, most of them children. Bok'eh was terrified of it.

Poor Mamma got over the worst of the dysentery, but was not really back to normal for six months and she never did the washing again.

A new bamboo building was built to house a sewing room where Japanese uniforms were made on hand-operated Singer sewing machines, some ancient. When Mamma was discharged from the hospital and after a short rest in the barracks, she went to work in the sewing room. She was an excellent dressmaker, as was Leida, who was also put to work in there.

The uniforms were cut by a Japanese man and the women had to sit for long hours turning the small sewing machines and ended the day with aching arms and sore backs. Bok'eh had told the women there would be extra little treats for making the uniforms, like soap, sugar and better food but this was a lie.

Later, one of the women complained about the amount of time they spent at their sewing machines making Japanese uniforms and where was our "pay"? Bok'eh went into a rage wanting to know how we dared ask for extras. "You could just be eating rice. How would you like that?" he said. No-one dared broach the question again and the uniforms continued to get made.

Other women had to knit socks or stockings for the Japs from white knitting cotton. Women who were unable to do any work because of bad health or other disabilities – as well as hospital patients who could sit up – had to embroider badges.

During the rainy season even the landgirls like me had to make button holes in the uniforms. The uniforms were made of striped material and I had to sit, day in and day out, for many hours making the cursed button holes. My eyes ached and watered and I saw stars and stripes from staring at the striped material.

Of course my head started aching again. Sitting on a hard narrow bamboo bench without a back for many hours made our backs ache like mad. How I hated that job. The Japs certainly had cheap labour and illegal labour at that. But who was there to do anything about it? Nobody in the whole wide world knew that 1700 women and children and a few men were imprisoned in a shabby camp called Kampili.

Then there was another job we land girls had to do. We had to pound rice to flour with a long, round wooden pole in a large deep wooden mortar. I found it very hard work. My arms ached like mad and I got huge blisters on the palms of my hands.

The rice flour was used to make bread, which was really a rare treat, so the sore arms and blisters were worthwhile. Even if we had no butter, the bread which we got on rare occasions tasted delicious.

A pig farm was established, well away from all the buildings. A group of women had to tend the pigs, which were solely for Japanese consumption. These animals got much better food than we did. Their food was trucked in from the Japanese army kitchens in Makassar.

The swine were also much better housed. They lived on wooden floors, while we only had a dirt floor under our feet. A new well was dug by the pig quarters especially for them, while we were pouring mud on our bodies.

The farm started off with a small number of pigs but gradually the number increased and the women found themselves looking after a great number. They became very fond of them.

Whenever Japanese VIPs came, they always inspected the pigs, which had to be washed because they had to be impeccably clean. The pigs were fattened, then slaughtered and sent to the Japs. None of the meat came our way.

For us, one thin kerbau (water buffalo), the size of a small donkey, had to be shared by the 1700 of us. We were supposed to get one kerbau a day, but that did not happen. Meat soon became a luxury and a forlorn memory.

Lies, who assisted Father Beltjens, the butcher priest, had a bad accident. She cut her hand during work at the butchery and got a massive infection. She was in great pain and was off work for more than six weeks. Lies could not look after her children, so Leida and I took one each.

Leida looked after Marianne and I took care of little Wietse. We bathed them, fed them and put them to bed. We also did the washing for Lies and her children.

During that time Leida and I had to go to our jobs, while the two little ones went to the camp creche.

We loved looking after these two delightful children. They were no trouble and it was a load off their mother's mind. Lies suffered a great deal but she never complained. Her cut thumb was ravaged by the infection and left it disfigured which meant she could not go back to the butchery. She was, in fact, very lucky to survive the infection.

17. The Pests

We were tormented by mosquitoes and many people fell ill with malaria, including Mamma and Leida, who contracted the frightful malaria tropica strain.

They were so ill and I had to look after two very sick patients with high fevers as well as little Lia. I wasn't in particularly good health myself with that pain in my abdomen all the time.

Luckily the malaria that Mamma and Leida had could be treated with quinine which at that time (1943) was still readily available. It was really effective and the two of them recovered fairly quickly, although they were quite weak for several weeks.

One thing was certain. We were living primitively and doing without plenty of essentials. But we could not do without mosquito nets. An urgent request was made to Bok'eh and a short time later a quantity of cheap, very thin material was delivered. People hurriedly set about sewing the nets and soon we all had one.

There was not enough for full-sized nets. The ones made were very low and just covered our bodies lying down. There was just enough to tuck the net in under the mat all around you, but you could not sit up. Never mind, at least we could now sleep without being eaten up by these little pests.

While the mosquitoes were mercifully kept at bay, we had no such luck with the bugs, mini beetle-type nuisances. They made their cosy little nests in the corners and we were plagued by the little horrors, which stank terribly. We had to de-bug our nets every day and wash them whenever there was soap and enough water.

If these two pests were not enough, they were joined by rats as big as kittens. How frightening they were. They kept us awake and I was absolutely terrified as these huge monsters made their nests inside the large, hollow bamboo of the barrack frame and gnawed their way through the knots. They also seemed to play games, chasing each other and squealing loudly along the roof above my head in the top bunk. They were always very noisy.

I was unable to sleep, not just because of the noise, but also because I was scared stiff. But in the end I was compelled to get used to the rats because I needed sleep very badly.

One night I was rudely and painfully awakened. I felt a sharp pain in the little finger of my left hand which lay beside me on the mat inside the mosquito net. To my horror, I saw a dark monster next to me and through the net had the tip of my finger between its fangs. This huge rat was hanging on to my hand.

I gave the most agonized scream and literally crashed down from the top bunk onto the dirt floor of our tiny cubicle. The rat let go of my finger and ran away when I screamed. I landed between the bottom bunks on which Lia and Mamma lay. It was a miracle I didn't break a leg or sustain any other injury, but I caused a great commotion, waking up most of the women and children in our barrack.

Poor Mamma had great difficulty calming me down and she allowed me to sleep in Lia's bunk. It was a very long time before I dared sleep in my top bunk again.

Oh, if Peter our tom cat was still around. The little ginger monster Leida and I had brought from Malino usually slept on my bunk during the day and for most of the night he went out on his tom cat business. We had become very attached to the lovely cat.

But one day Peter did not come back in the morning for his food. Leida and I went round the camp asking everyone without luck. Peter had disappeared without trace and we never found out what had happened to him. We were broken-hearted, but we didn't have time to mourn for long.

The Pests

Perhaps the biggest pest at Kampili was the flies. They were a real menace as well as a serious health hazard. The number of dysentery patients increased by the day, so Bok'eh organised a fly-catching drive. Everybody, except the old, sick and small children had to catch 100 flies a day.

With a bucket or a tin with some soapy water we set about this dirty job. We had to catch the flies with our hands and as there were so many, it was not difficult to catch your quota of 100. Even then, it didn't seem to make a great deal of difference.

One woman was appointed to receive the catch and she had to write our names down. Bok'eh was also present to check, then the bacteriologist, Dr Marseille, dumped the sodden mess into a bucket of disinfectant. The occupants of the barrack which had caught the most flies were rewarded with soap and sugar.

Unfortunately we in barrack 12 missed out on these highly prized goodies. We had to catch flies every day but the soap and sugar was only a one-off prize.

Surprise surprise, we were allowed to have a few lessons in the dining room. There were only a few textbooks teachers had managed to keep secretly and hardly any paper and pencils. But the teachers were wonderful women and very dedicated and they wanted to teach us whatever and whenever they could.

Although I was very tired, I enjoyed it. We were allowed little time for the school and it took place only after we'd finished our jobs. In the evening we had to water the vegetable garden which by then had been established.

But school seemed to be granted on a whim by Bok'eh and as a result it was often disrupted. If things were going well for the Japs we could have school but if things were going wrong, which happened more frequently as time went on, school was prohibited. We never knew from one day to the next what was going to happen.

The same with Bok'eh's mood, which fluctuated wildly. You knew that if he was in a good mood, the Japanese were doing alright in the war but if they were suffering, then we were likely to suffer. He would be very nervous, short-tempered and aggressive. Apparently he was petrified that if the war went too badly, he would have to go to the front and see some action. He didn't want that after the cushy life he had at Kampili.

Bok'eh was well fed and looked after by one or two boys and a few women who cooked for him. He always ate well and he never failed to let us know that he was the boss at all times and he alone had authority.

When he was in that mood you steered well clear of him, because he was liable to lash out and just bash someone up for the sake of it.

18. Terror from the Air

Suddenly during 1944, the allies started their air raids and we were constantly kept awake by the sound of bombardments in the area. They were usually during the night and filled the whole camp with terror and panic.

A bell was installed in front of the commandant's abode and a woman had to sit by the bell and raise the alarm by ringing the bell whenever the ominous droning of aircraft was heard.

As soon as the alarm sounded, we were ordered to evacuate the barracks and head for the nearest gutter.

First it was the mosquitoes that kept us awake at night and then the rats. Now it was the air raids, which were very frequent. After nights of little or no sleep we felt exhausted, but we couldn't sleep during the day because we all had work.

These raids made us frightened not only for ourselves but also for our loved ones elsewhere.

People estimated that the bombardments were on Makassar and surrounding areas and we often thought of Pappa.

We had no idea where he was, although we all thought of the men still being in Makassar and feared for their safety. We didn't know it but by this time Pappa was a prisoner of war in Batavia (Jakarta).

19. Weather Woes

The weather was very hot, there hadn't been any rain for some time and our wells were drying up. The dust was terrible, settling on everyone and everything. We were dependent solely on rain for our water and the shortage was of great concern. People became despondent and then they started to panic.

Whenever the wells ran dry, including the one by the central kitchen, the land girls had to form a human chain from the kitchen to a spring outside the barbed wire fence. Under the cruel sun standing barefoot on the burning sand, we girls had to pass bucket after bucket of water one way and receive empty ones from the kitchen toward the spring again.

Sometimes when the sand became too hot for my feet I would scoop a little water from the bucket and sprinkle it on the sand. It was a merciful relief but it only lasted a short time. I couldn't do it often because I would have been told off for wasting the precious water, so for most of the time I had to hop from one foot to the other.

This work was very boring and to make it more interesting I used to make up stories and fantasies which I relayed to my neighbours and they seemed to enjoy them. The work also made me very tired and I suffered bad headaches.

But God must have pitied us because at the most critical time of the drought it started to rain, earlier than usual. Now we had an abundance of this precious, life-sustaining substance. Even though we had little else, we were very grateful to have the water.

One day there was a terrible thunderstorm. I was sitting on my bunk and to my horror I saw a fireball the size of a football racing through our barrack. It flew in through the front opening, raced along the length of the centre aisle in between the rows of bunks on both sides and disappeared out the back opening. It was an amazing sight and we were very lucky nobody was in its path.

The weather always affected us one way or another, because we were housed in such flimsy buildings and we had no facilities to rely on and no proper protection.

Shortly after that terrible thunderstorm a wind gust ripped the roof off our dining room. The fragile structure collapsed and very slowly sank to the ground and it was fortunate people had time to get out. Our barrack was shaking dangerously but kept upright. That was the end of our dining room and we did not get another one.

The worst thing to happen in that storm was that the storage shed also collapsed. There was rice, sugar, salt, onions and wood for the kitchen fires stored in that shed. In torrential rain people raced over to save what they could but it was all bad news for us. The onions rotted and after a month the rice became musty and inedible.

This was a real disaster as our diet was already very poor. Very little meat, sometimes a bit of fish which was half rotten and often hardly any vegetables. For several weeks we received little sugar, which was a disaster when we had to eat musty rice porridge without it. The result was that many people fell ill.

After the storms the barracks had become perilous. The buildings could no longer take the battering of the freakish weather conditions. They were rebuilt at high speed by natives with whom we were forbidden to communicate. During the rebuilding we were housed in all sorts of available sheds.

I got some deep, festering sores on my ankles and the inside of my knees as a result of the wet weather. They became very pussy and I was plagued by flies trying to get at them. There was nothing to put on the sores, so I plugged them up with mud, of which there was a plentiful supply.

I was not the only one to suffer festering sores. There was a middle-aged American woman who was muscular and very strong. She was a Christian Science missionary, I think. One day I happened to be sitting next to her and I noticed an ugly, festering wound on her foot. The foot was very swollen and had turned purple. It made me shudder and when I mentioned it she said: "God will heal it."

I greatly admired her for her faith. She was not living in our barrack and I didn't see her for some time but that ugly sore did heal, as did mine after a long time.

I developed 'dropsy', a mild form of beri-beri which is a lack of vitamin B2. Dropsy causes fluid to collect in cavities or tissues of the body and it made me feel very uncomfortable. If I looked up to the sky I felt dizzy and if I wasn't careful I would lose my balance.

Our toothbrushes had worn out and toothpaste had long since been used up. As toothbrushes we used a fibrous type of nut, and ash from the kitchen fires made excellent toothpaste. With these two substitutes we could do quite a good job. We had very little soap, although sporadically we were given a tiny piece. We cherished it.

There was only one dentist in the camp and she had tools and a very limited supply of materials. She did not have any anaesthetic and she had to use her tools manually as we had no power. Surgery and waiting room were one, so patients waiting their turn were subjected to watching the dentist at work and suffering the screams of the poor patients.

When we came to Kampili, I was wearing primitive clogs made of a very light type of wood. They were just a sole with a low heel and a thin rubber strap across the toes. The straps were fastened on either side of the soles with tiny nails, like a dressmaker's pins. These flimsy clogs did not last long, with firstly the nails coming away. I hammered them back in repeatedly but in the end the thin rubber straps broke and the soles just disintegrated. As I had no other footwear, I had to walk barefoot from then on.

When we were evacuated to Malino in January 1942 I was not yet 14 and I had not had my first period. During our stay in Malino I did not get one and during the years in Kampili when I reached 17-and-a-half I had still to experience my first period. It was a shock when I did get my first period after the war because I thought I was going to bleed to death.

Mamma and Leida's periods stopped altogether during the war, which was a blessing, really.

Some women suffered heavy periods and there was no way to get relief without asking Bok'eh to get some sanitary pads. It was humiliating having to ask this man for these and it seemed as if he enjoyed our humiliation. However, on his next trip to Makassar, Bok'eh brought back some thick grey-coloured brushed cotton material similar to the stuff which was used to wash the floors before the war. But it did the trick for those poor, suffering women.

We always seemed to be in embarrassing situations. Our clothes were just about falling off our backs and we desperately needed new ones.

At last, big boxes containing second-hand garments were delivered by truck and we had to queue up and were allowed one or two items each. There were people who recognised their own clothes from before the war. Mamma, Leida and I didn't recognise any of ours among the assortment but we were grateful to get one or two garments.

Working on the land like a coolie in the blazing tropical sun caused heavy perspiring. The land girls really needed more clothes because our clothes wore out very quickly. I didn't even have a clean change.

Again, we faced this humiliating situation of having to ask the camp commandant for something. After a time some bales of cheap flimsy material arrived and were delivered to the sewing room. The ladies were ordered to sew a hansop – a one-piece garment of shorts and sleeveless top with a square neckline – for each one of us land girls. A hansop is very simple to make but the sewing women also had to keep up their quota of uniforms. Tough going until the hansops were finished.

I was thrilled with my new hansop in a pretty lemon colour but as it was cheap material it hung on my body like a limp and crumpled rag after only a couple of washings and the colour faded.

There were some harrowing stories of people cracking up at Kampili. One afternoon when most of us were lying down for a short rest to get out of the scorching sun, the shimmering silence was suddenly pierced by the agonising screams of a child outside our barrack.

Within seconds, everyone flew outside and raced to where the screams were coming from. There they were confronted by a woman who was beating her young daughter on the head with a wooden clog. The women restrained her and led mother and distraught child inside.

While they comforted the little girl the mother began to cry and between sobs she said she never intended to hit her daughter but her nerves had snapped. She lived in our barrack with the girl and another little boy and she was not a bad mother. She loved her children very much but things had got on top of her.

She was a very robust looking woman and it took the women quite some time to calm her and her daughter down, while the son just looked on, not understanding why his mother had acted in such a violent manner.

There was one death at Kampili caused by someone just 'giving up'. One, a 38-year-old woman, Mrs JMH Koekkelkoren died on December 10 1944 from what was described as a psychological disorder. Life was tough and I'm surprised there were not more examples of that, although there were often problems after the war when marriages came apart as a direct result of the deprivations both partners suffered during the hostilities.

20. Japanese Nerves

High-ranking Japanese army officers regularly visited us and before these VIP visits we were ordered to sweep the dirt floor inside our barracks, the area around them and the camp terrain. They provided us with cheap brooms for this dirty job.

I hated this useless, boring job that made me breathe in the awful dust and made my head ache. When the sweeping was done, we had to bathe and put clean clothes on – that's if you had any clean clothes.

Then the land girls were ordered to line up on both sides of the drive leading from the main gate to the commandant's house and office. There we had to stand, barefooted in the blazing sun sometimes for hours, to wait for the arrival of the Japanese hierarchy.

They arrived in chauffeur-driven cars once owned by Dutch people who were now their prisoners. As they approached us, a woman would shout in Dutch for us to stand to attention, then to bow – from the waist of course. We had to do it whether we liked it or not, because the risk of being punished for disobedience was not worth it.

Ino, the officer who visited us in the doctor's house in Malino, turned up one day at Kampili. He walked through our barracks hunting for books, which he ordered to be handed in to be burned. Religious tomes again escaped the purge but not cookbooks this time. They were even more useless than before but in they went. This odious creature was obsessed about our reading books. We had to work for our living and we mustn't be idle, was his message. We worked very hard all day, so there was no time to be idle, let alone have the chance to read.

At this time there was a lot of war activity. We heard heavy booming noises at a distance, which people presumed to be coming from the sea. The bombardments by the Allies also continued and we now saw American planes flying directly over our camp.

One day when I was working and sweating in the fields, I saw planes flying in the direction of Makassar and then I heard bombs being dropped. I got goose pimples and felt very uneasy, thinking always of Pappa and all the other people living there. Several days later the planes returned and again hit Makassar. We tried to be happy at these times because they were Allied planes doing the damage, but the happiness was tinged with horrible feelings in the pits of our stomachs thinking of the things and the people we left behind in Makassar.

We used to sing Dutch songs while working in the fields to keep our spirits up but soon the Japanese put a stop to that. What did they think we were doing? Plotting rebellion with our singing?

Bok'eh became very nervous and erratic. Every day he gave different orders. Although our school was prohibited, the primary school could continue but in a different place. Lia had now started school and the children were spread all over the camp in little groups so as not to attract the attention of the Japs.

Then after some time, the high school students were allowed some lessons again for a few hours in the afternoon – when we'd finished our work on the land. However, we had to sit on mats in the open in baking temperatures. Our teachers remained wonderfully dedicated, keeping going in extremely trying circumstances with amazing energy and determination. This was particularly difficult because the teachers also had regular jobs and some had children to be cared for.

I had great respect for these women and I will always be grateful for what they taught, which was not only academic knowledge but also – and this was very important, particularly at Kampili – attitude, courage, patience, tolerance and perseverance.

By now, with our diet getting worse by the day, many people became weak and had less resistance to dysentery, malaria and other potential killers at the camp. People, including children, died. Others became depressed and an atmosphere of gloom and despair hung over the camp. Another woman, aged 54, died in 1944 when she simply gave up the ghost and decided she'd had enough. If you want to die enough, as these poor women did, there is not a lot you can do except watch them fade and die and the conditions under which we lived made it very easy to succeed with a death wish.

The Japanese were very scared of catching a contagious disease. Because bacillus dysentery is very contagious, sufferers were isolated in a barrack ward way out in the vegetable garden. For these people it was a miserable time. Nobody, not even family members, was allowed to visit them and it was very distressing, particularly for children, being separated from their mothers.

But it was also necessary because in our condition one could easily become infected. The Japs particularly thought it necessary no matter how much hardship it caused, because they were petrified of this vicious disease.

A person near us caught another very contagious disease and was promptly isolated. I can't remember what the disease was but it was much worse than dysentery and as a precautionary measure, people in our barrack, including us and others who had been close to her – about 100 people – had to move to a separate barrack. This barrack and some latrines behind it and the bathroom next to it, were roped off. We were the untouchables.

We had strict orders not to go beyond the rope and not to have any contact with people on the other side. Our food and drinking water were placed by the rope in front of the barrack. The receptacles for our food and water were disinfected and kept for our use only and we had to clean our bathroom and latrines every day with disinfectant.

This was in the monsoon season and every day it rained cats and dogs and it was most depressing. It was like a prison within a prison and we were outcasts with nothing to do except clean and disinfect the place. We had nothing to read and it nearly drove us crazy. But our sacrifice had to be worth it if the whole camp wasn't to be wiped out by disease.

I can't remember exactly how long we were in quarantine but it was several months and it was certainly an immense relief when at long last we could move back to our own barrack. Bad as that was, it was paradise compared with the quarantine block.

The land girls had to pick vegetables in all weathers and in the monsoon season we had to wade waistdeep through the mud, with the muck oozing between our toes. Consequently I got a nasty skin infection between my toes called kutu air – or athlete's foot – with deep raw cuts. This was sheer misery but there was not much I could do about it except try to keep them dry as much as possible, which was impossible with no footwear.

21. Light Relief

Amid all the misery of death, disease, anguish, fear and hunger, there was the rare treat of a show, during which we'd manage to forget our troubles for a few hours.

We'd be entertained by some very enterprising women who could actually make us laugh. I particularly remember Tine, who imitated Maurice Chevalier. She was tall and thin and had a deep voice and she had us all in stitches singing and mimicking the popular French singer. She was dressed just like him with hat at an angle on her head. The most successful song was Ma Louise – "every bird seems to twitter Louise, can't it be true someone like you could love me" – which she performed in the Chevalier style with the nasal accent. Tine was a real artist among us.

There was a ballet performance by some teenage boys, which was absolutely hilarious. To see those gangly lads prancing around awkwardly, their dainty arms and legs sticking out of dainty ballerina costumes made especially by some clever dressmakers, was the funniest show I had ever seen.

We had one musical show in which many teenagers performed. There were a prince, a princess and court attendants. Leida and I also participated but we had only very minor roles. The costumes were made by the mothers from a variety of cast-off bits of material. As we did not have anything ourselves, we had to go around asking for some odds and ends. Mamma was very clever and from the scraps, she made very attractive costumes for Leida and me.

The shows were many months apart but they were a welcome relief from the tiresome heavy daily workload, anxiety, sickness, gloomy atmosphere and endless dreary isolation and deprivation. They were a real tonic.

Christmas 1943 was a quiet affair as we had nothing to be happy about. All we could do was pray. There were about 100 nuns in the camp who all lived in one barrack and the Roman Catholics all had a night mass with an improvised altar. There was also a service for the Protestants.

On New Year's Eve we were treated to a funny review of the past year's events. We were gathered in the church shed and a small choir under the guidance of our own Olga sang Russian songs. Olga accompanied them on the old piano which had arrived from somewhere – obviously looted.

But there was no food or drink and we went to bed at the usual time as soon as it grew dark because we had no lights. What would 1944 bring, apart from my 16th birthday?

22. The New Year

In 1944 a lot of bad and sad things happened. The Japanese were getting more and more agitated and to start with we were not allowed to have any more gatherings. We were not even allowed to be together with a few people.

From now on we had to learn to obey orders given in Japanese. Up to this time the orders were always given in Dutch by the heads of the different work groups. Now these women had to learn to shout the orders in the enemy's language.

And we were drilled like soldiers to stand to attention, bow, back to attention, at ease and dismiss. There were endless roll calls to get us used to the orders shouted in Japanese.

High-ranking Japanese officers visited us again. Some were from the Kenpeitai, the Japanese Gestapo or military police. These Japs always had to inspect the pig farm, the sewing room and the polyclinic, where I had my appendix removed. And they had to be opened in a hurry, no matter what time of day it was.

One day when there was such a visit and inspection, the Kenpeitai took two American missionary women back to Makassar with them. One of these women was the muscular, middle-aged woman Miss Seely.

The neurotic commandant was becoming increasingly irrational and agitated. Out of the blue he told us we were not allowed any more school. Instead we had to work on the land in the morning starting at 7am as well as the afternoon right through till 6pm. This was very tough and I was always exhausted after a long day working on the land. It was also soul destroying. There was nothing to stimulate the brain, hacking away in the infertile hard Celebes soil.

Bok'eh was very short tempered, resulting in many punishments. One form of punishment often meted out was to stand in the blazing sun for hours on end in front of his office. You could be punished for a variety of reasons, even trumped-up charges, just to satisfy him or possibly also to show us that he was the boss and could do with us what he wanted.

He was a master at handing out beatings with his trusty stick, or smacking a woman on the face with his hand or boxing the ears. He could deliver a mighty strong blow, often knocking his victim to the ground. We always felt sorry for the recipient of a beating and always lived in fear of being next.

I particularly remember one such horrendous beating. It was in the afternoon at the hottest part of that awful day when everything was quiet and everyone was sluggish because of the heat. The silence was suddenly broken by agonising, piercing screams. Immediately everyone was jolted out of apathy and women from all over the camp raced to where the screams were coming from.

Lily Gravelotte, our cheerful barrack crier, was the victim on this occasion as Bok'eh beat her all over her back with his stick in an attack that lasted all of two minutes. Blow after blow hit Lily and with each one she let out the horrific screams that still haunt me today.

When the revolting, sweating Bok'eh had had enough, he gave Lily a kick and walked back into his office. We carried Lily in and laid her carefully on her bunk. She was a broken person in an awful mess.

After some time Lily gave us the whole story. Poor Lily had been beaten up by Bok'eh because she had been unable to unload big, heavy sacks of rice from a truck which had just arrived. The very heavy sacks had to be lifted off the truck and carried to the rebuilt storage shed some distance away. Lily tried to explain to Bok'eh that before the war she had had an operation on one arm and therefore was unable to carry heavy things. She apparently showed him the scar to prove she was not making it up, but the brute flew into a rage, jerked her around and took to her with his stick.

Tropical paradise . . . Gerarda, aged 8, is pictured with her mother Louisa and sister Leida (right) in the peaceful 1930s in the Dutch East Indies.

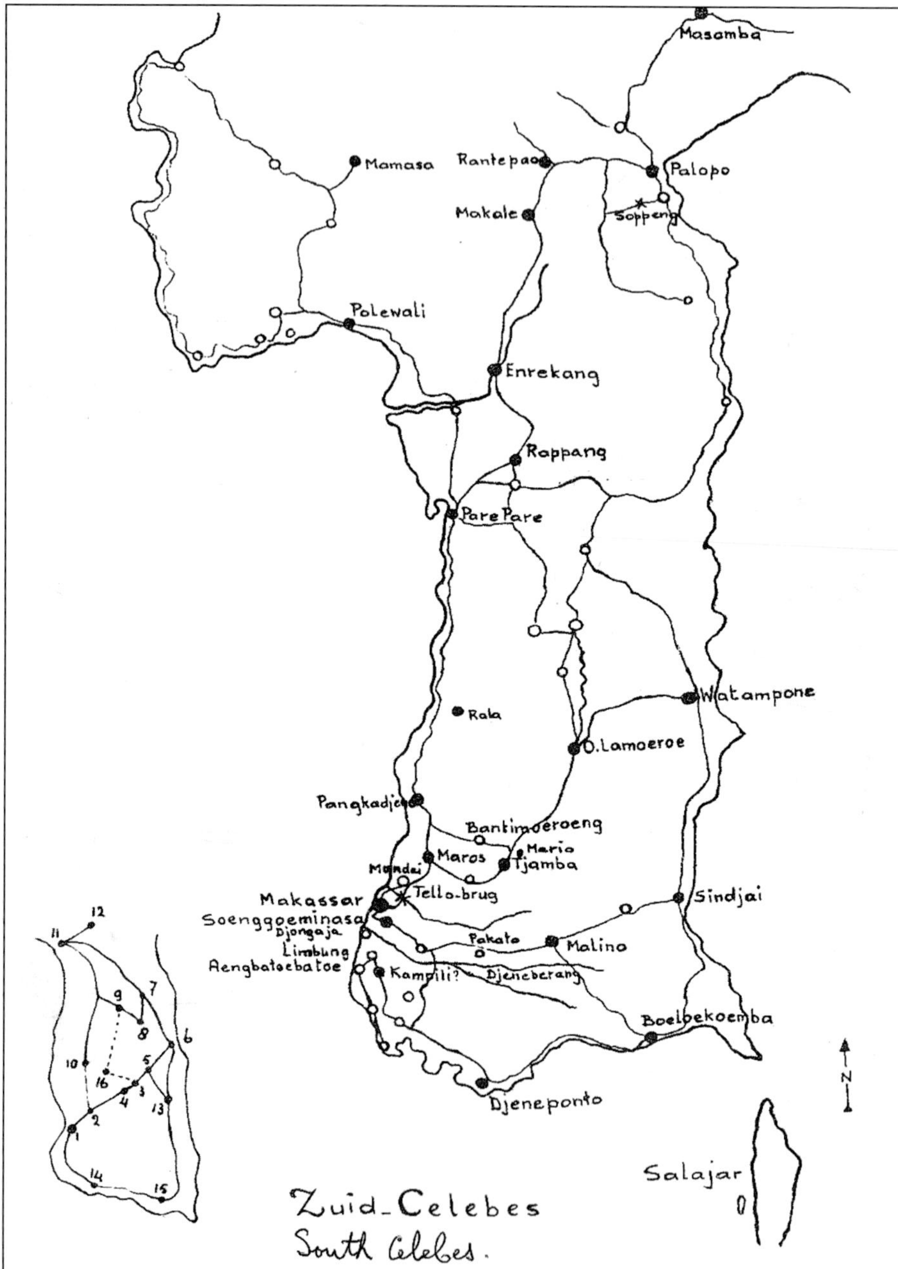

South Celebes (now known as Sulawesi) . . . Makassar is at bottom left, Kampili just below and inland, and Malino in the middle of the island.

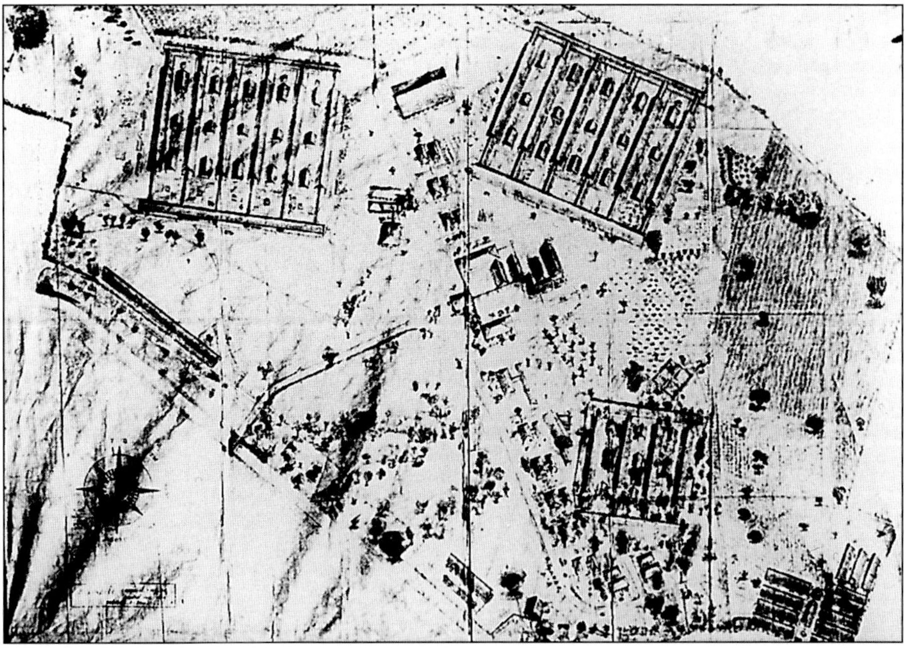

Kampili . . . the Koning's barrack in complex B is top left, complex A on the right and complex C rear at the bottom. In the middle is the Commandant's house, the central kitchen and the hospital.

Another view of Kampili, with complex B to the left, complex A on the right and some of the little houses which held the Ambon people.

'Uncle' Bok'eh . . . 'that's him handing out sweets to the children on the Queen's birthday at Boskamp'.

Queen Wilhelmina's birthday . . . Gerarda is on the right in this picture, taken on August 31, 1945. These two photos were taken by a Japanese photographer and given to Gerarda.

Landgirls . . . 'we looked a happy enough group here, but this belies the hardships we faced in the fields'.

After the inferno . . . a Japanese admiral (left) and Bok'eh the morning after Kampili was destroyed, July 17 1945.

The nightmare is over . . . Pappa, Mamma and Lia in Sydney, September 1946.

Sydneyside . . . Gerarda (left) and Leida with Pappa in Sydney.

Family gathering . . . Auckland 1983 when Leida visited from The Netherlands. From left, Pappa, Mamma, Gerarda and husband Oliver and Leida.

Lily was lying on her stomach groaning. She was obviously in great pain and deep shock and was very white. We were horrified and also numb with shock at seeing the bloody, deep cuts on the poor woman's back. Poor, poor Lily. She was in the wrong place at the wrong time. The bastard had lost his temper again.

Even now I can still see the bloodied cuts all over her back. I could not understand how any man could inflict such injury and pain on another person, least of all how a man could do that to an innocent, defenseless woman.

The group of women whose unfortunate job it usually was to unload trucks delivering drums of kerosene and oil, as well as rice and other supplies, suffered many injuries, but the most common one was collapsed arches. This was really no work for women, but there was nobody else to do the job unless Bok'eh and his poor little assistant lent a hand, and of course the commandant was not going to let that happen.

Another tough job was the sewing room where Mamma and Leida worked terribly long hours. Sitting behind a hand-operated sewing machine for hours on end was becoming too much for a lot of women, as it was also for the women who had to knit men's socks and stockings of white knitting cotton.

None of these women had decent chairs. They had to sit on hard bamboo seats without backs and as our diet was very poor, not only did their bodies suffer, their eyes were also strained to the limit.

Many people fell ill suffering all sorts of ailments. The worst was probably lack of vitamins which showed up at first in a kind of mouth infection and by continuing without important vitamins, an epidemic of a kind of dropsy followed.

The symptoms were swollen legs and frightening weight increases. These patients were put on a saltless diet and weighed every day. The ailment seemed to decrease to be replaced by beriberi, another disease caused by the lack of the desired vitamins, in this case B.

The result was very serious because beriberi causes legs and fingertips to become numb. If this spread to the rest of the body it could end up with the victim not being able to walk.

Something had to be done. The pigs were always given the outside, vitamin-rich film of rice, but now this layer was also mixed into the beriberi patients' porridge. The rest of us got bananas, even if they were rotten.

Sugar, which is always important in one's diet, was also scarce. I suffered spells of feeling faint and trembling and Mamma gave me a tiny amount of our vital but inadequate sugar ration. This helped me for a short time only but I could not have any more sugar because that would have been unfair on

Mamma, Leida and Lia. It was a really wretched time for all of us but for mothers it was particularly worrying.

To cap it all, there was a rumour going around the camp that we would be transported to another place. Remembering that a similar rumour while we were in Malino unfortunately became reality, this rumour filled us all with dread.

This particular scare, apparently spread by Bok'eh, turned out to be false.

23. Beautiful Night Skies

The Allied Forces were becoming very active. There were frequent bombardments now and when the alarm bell sounded we had to run to the gutter by our barrack as fast as we could. During air raids, which were mostly at night, we could be spending many hours in the open gutter.

Often the night was exceptionally beautiful, with millions and millions of stars twinkling brightly, while everything around us was in deep darkness. With a full moon the picture above us was even more spectacular. The sky was so beautiful and peaceful that when gazing at the wonderful spectrum and when there were no droning of planes and no bomb explosions, you could almost forget, temporarily at least, the sheer misery we were living in day in and day out.

One day, two Japanese doctors arrived with all their gear. They set up a surgery, not to treat sick people but to examine every one of us. One doctor was in charge of all blood examinations and he had a lot of tiny glass plates, one for each person's blood sample. The other doctor listened to lungs, checked heart, spleen, liver and all the other organs.

I found this examination excruciatingly embarrassing and I was very frightened too, when this alien little man wearing glasses with thick lens put his hands all over my body, lingering over my breasts. Fortunately there were also a few of our own nurses on hand with this mass examination, a condition laid down by our doctors.

I was greatly relieved when it was all over but to my horror I was told to go back to see the doctors. I was absolutely petrified. What on earth were they going to do to me now? And why me?

When I got there I was told that my blood sample had been spoiled by flies, so they had to get a fresh sample. Another needle. I shuddered. I had really had more than enough of needles.

We all wondered why these examinations were necessary. Later, we realised that the aim of these Japanese doctors was purely scientific, gathering statistics on everyone's nutritional condition but of course we never found out the results, and our diet did not improve.

It actually deteriorated. We had to work the hard, infertile soil under the cruel sun to produce vegetables for 1700 people. The production of vegetables was very changeable and sometimes, if we were lucky, it was sufficient. But more often, we had little or no vegetables for weeks on end.

Behind the latrines of our six barracks complex B was the garden for kassbi or ketela, a tuberous plant. A group of teenage girls, including me, had to work this garden and one of our tasks was to fertilise these plants with the contents of the sewer pit. We had to scoop the muck out and pour it around the ketela plants.

One day I felt so hungry I pinched a small tuber and ate it raw there and then. Luckily I was not caught in the act by Bok'eh because I would probably have got a thrashing. But I was punished. I suffered excruciating stomach cramps and diarrhoea for some days and the trouble was that I could not report sick because it wasn't dysentery.

Everybody who fell ill had to report to Bok'eh, who always wanted to know the whole story and then he would decide if a person was sick and needed a rest or whether it was a feigned case. He certainly was not stupid and worse luck, he had a fantastic memory. He would have branded me a thief and punished me.

24. The Pits

The sewer pits rapidly filled again despite our fertilising efforts. Before long they were filled to the brim.

So everyone, except old and sick people and children, had to set to and scoop out the revolting, stinking muck. A small tin nailed to a long bamboo pole served as a dipper with which we had to scoop out the muck and pour it into a few high square kerosene tins. When the two tins were full we had to carry them to the vegetable garden behind the latrines and pour the filthy muck around the plants. They had tried to grow banana trees but this experiment was a total flop. But still, we dutifully fertilised them as well as the vegetables.

To keep tabs on everyone and make sure nobody cheated, a little old lady sitting on a rickety bamboo stool, kept the record on a piece of paper with a pencil stub. It was incredible that there were always people who tried to cheat and get out of doing their fair share. After all, everyone had contributed with filling up the sewer pits, so they should be willing to help get rid of it. Human nature dictates that there will always be the cheats, or attempted cheats, but they couldn't get away with it. Despite the old lady toting up our efforts, Bok'eh would have known. He always knew what was going on and often it seemed as if he knew every one of us individually. The cheats would not have prospered.

For every person the quota was 20 kerosene tins to be filled and emptied on the garden. We also carried out Mamma's quota because she was not feeling strong enough. It was awfully hot that day and there was a hazy shimmer over the land. The stench coming off the human waste was unbearable and flies were a constant menace and an acute health hazard. And if this wasn't enough, there was the nauseating, wriggling mass of maggots – millions of them.

Leida and I had no footwear left, so we had to perform a kind of step-dance to avoid the revolting things. Sixty of these kerosene tins was really a heck of a lot for two teenage girls, in particular for me having had that big operation. We could not have a rest because we had to work non-stop so others could have their turn.

After finally finishing our quota, we felt filthy and totally exhausted. We took a long time scrubbing ourselves as clean as we could with the little soap we had left. Events like this one stick with me and I can still see this revolting scene in my mind and still smell the stench.

Living so close together in such primitive conditions had its problems. Our neighbour Lies had a cubicle with three bunks, two of which were bottom ones. Next to Lies was a mother and her two young sons, who had a bottom bunk and two top ones where the boys slept – one of them above Lies.

This boy kept a tin on his bed which he used as a chamber pot during the night and one night after the boy had relieved himself, he accidentally knocked the tin over. The urine seeped through the thin mat and through the rough bamboo bunk base and like a miniature waterfall it ran down onto the sleeping Lies below. But Lies, good sport that she was, got up without being angry, had a good wash in the dark, cleaned up her bed and went back to sleep.

There was another similar incident which we found rather funny. Two women in another barrack were outside talking as it was growing dark, when they felt a fine spray, which they thought to be water sprinkling over them. But it was not raining. They looked up and noticed the fine spray was coming from inside the barrack through the thin bamboo wall. Puzzled, they went inside to investigate.

They could not believe their eyes. The source of the spray was a bamboo tube which had been pushed through the barrack wall and on the inside end of the tube, on a top bunk, stood a little boy who was peeing through the tube. His small penis fitting nicely into the tube and he was quite pleased with his little invention.

25. Trench Warfare

The aerial bombardments seemed to be coming closer to Kambili. Trenches were dug for us in a great hurry by natives to be used as shelter during air raids. Some trenches were left open like the one near our barrack, while others were covered with tree trunks with more earth piled on the trees.

I soon worked out that these covered shelters were potential death traps because the tree trunks forming the ceiling of the shelters were sure to be shaken loose during a bombardment and, together with the heap of soil, could collapse onto the people sheltering inside them.

Those shelters were very low and narrow and one could not stand up in them. You had to crawl inside and sit down on the dirt floor and lean up against the damp side with legs pulled up. I was very glad that our shelter was open.

During the monsoon season both types of shelters flooded. As ours was open it would fill up much quicker and we could almost swim in it.

We thought it was strange that we had air raid shelters and that we always had to go into them, because we thought that our Allies knew there were women and children in our camp, so we would not be their target. Much later, we found out the reason, though it was just as well we had no idea of the real situation at that time.

One night the whole sky lit up in brilliant colours of green, pink and yellowish-white. It was a still, dark night with just the stars twinkling above us. There were no bombardments at that time, just this magnificent spectre of light. We assumed it to be a meteor fragment hitting our planet or a comet. Whatever it was it was very spectacular and awe-inspiring, which couldn't be said for the bombing raids we were experiencing.

Another time during a night air raid while sitting in our trench full of people, I started to hum a tune which, according to some people was the tune played by the ship's orchestra when the Titanic went down. I didn't even know which tune it was and nor did I have any idea about the connection. I didn't even know I was humming what was really an unfortunate choice considering our situation. Someone sitting near Mamma said angrily: "Can't you stop that child?" I think it was because my nerves had had a real battering and I didn't really know what I was doing.

The bombardments executed by the American bombers happened more frequently and they also seemed to come closer to our camp. They were really giving Makassar hell.

I was grateful that I had learned to pray. I prayed a lot during those horrible years and I was sure God would hear my call and that we would be liberated from that awful dump and brought back into a peaceful, civilised world again, hopefully with Pappa. All we knew of Pappa was that he was taken prisoner early in 1942 and it was difficult in our circumstances to believe he could still be alive.

Very unexpectedly, one day we were allowed to swim in the muddy canal running along the front of our camp – but we had to do our jobs first.

We were kept under strict supervision while splashing around in the filthy muddy water. Further upstream we could see little Indonesian boys bathing their water buffaloes in the canal.

There was also a village not far away and turds drifted down past us. But this could not dampen our pleasure as swimming in the canal was really a treat. I had an old woollen swimsuit which I found in a closet at the doctor's bungalow in Malino.

There was another treat. On rare occasions we were given little white yeast balls. These were used to put in the middle of some cooked rice and wrapped in banana leaves (when we could get them) and left to ferment. The end product was called tapai, which with a little bit of sugar (rarely available) really tasted delicious.

One young, very intelligent woman with a university degree, used to make tapai in her porcelain chamber pot. The pot was quite big, so she had a lot of tapai, too much for her and her children. This generous woman then shared her chamber pot-made tapai with others who could not make any, which included us and in return Mamma gave her all our yeast balls. All you had to do was forget the tapai was made in a chamber pot.

26. Unable to Cope

The Kenpeitai paid us a visit again and when they left took some other women with them. They were away quite some time and when they were finally returned to our camp, along with the two American missionaries taken away earlier, they were in a bad condition.

They were not allowed to talk about their ordeal, but we did hear the Americans, including our little muscular friend Miss Seely, were locked in a cell for nine weeks. We all assumed everyone who went with the Kenpeitai was tortured, although what it wanted to know and what the women could tell them, nobody knows.

After a while Miss Seely started acting in a very strange way, no doubt brought on by her weeks locked up. She walked around the camp singing and professing her religion. Then she walked through some of the barracks clapping her hands, rocking her head and waving. All the time she kept on smiling and singing: "The victory of the Lord is here." They had taken her Bible and hymn book away.

Then the poor woman went literally berserk. She sang, banged on the walls and made wild gestures all the time. They had to lock her up in a little brick building called the 'tronk' – a secure unit obviously used frequently when the camp was a TB sanatorium – and she was so wild and strong that she nearly broke out and two people had to restrain her. It was terribly sad that her faith could not save her. I cannot remember what happened to her, but I hope they did manage to calm her down eventually.

Other women became completely introverted and isolated. I remember one young mother with a little boy who just gave up. She was lying on her back in her bunk all day, staring up at the bottom of the bunk above her. She was taken to the little women's hospital while someone in her barrack looked after her child. Fortunately she came out of it after the war when she was reunited with her husband who had been a prisoner in the civilian men's camp at Pare Pare.

This poor woman was not the only one either. Everybody felt sorry for those women who were unable to cope and there were plenty of kind and understanding people who would help and try to get them over their depression.

We all suffered fits of depression and mine were largely brought on by my missing Pappa, my books and my piano – and the mind-numbingly boring existence out in the fields.

However, towards the end of 1944 a long, narrow and very flimsy bamboo structure was built in the cow meadow. It had a row of tiny spaces where some bamboo tables and benches sat on the dirt floor.

Then it was announced that this building was to be our school. They even brought some blackboards, which the Japs would have pinched from somewhere.

We had no idea why all of a sudden we were being blessed with this privilege. Of course we still had to work, but school was a highly prized sort of beacon at the end of our work day and for me it was a real treat because I loved school and always did well.

With little in the way of equipment Sister Geraldine, Mrs van Goor, Mrs Chabot and Mrs Joustra worked wonders. I remember a maths class with Sister Geraldine when the weather turned really ugly. The thunder rolled menacingly and the lightning was so sharp and fierce it was quite frightening. Then one almighty lightning bolt flashed which was worse than the others and poor Sister Geraldine was just as frightened as the rest of us. She said: "Oh dear me" and made a frantic sign of the cross. I was terrified but I took great comfort in having her in that little room with me.

We had to endure really horrendous storms in that period and living in such flimsy buildings we had little protection from the elements. It was a miracle nobody was killed or badly injured during these storms.

During one storm we were dealt a terrible blow when our latrines were flattened. This was really too much. We had to make do with a drastically reduced number of loos. It was a real disaster.

Natives were engaged to rebuild the loos and it took them quite some time. They did not seem to be in any particular hurry and looking back you can't really blame them. This was probably one of the very few jobs they had during the years of the Japanese occupation, so they were stringing it out as long as possible. Mind you, it's difficult to know whether they got paid for the work and if they didn't there wasn't a lot they could do about it, such was life under the Japanese.

27. Dogfights Above Kampili

Our Allies were stepping up their air attacks. There were now many heavy bombardments, in particular during the night when the moon waxed. Those bombs must have caused horrendous injuries and damage whether they hit their targets or not, and their targets seemed to be closer and closer to Kampili.

Why were they coming closer? We found out the reason much later when we were their target.

One day when working outside the camp compound with a group of girls we heard a Japanese plane. You could tell a Jap plane because it sounded like a coffee grinder. American planes had a smooth droning sound. Shortly after we heard the short, sharp bursts of anti-aircraft guns, then a second plane came into view. It was an American plane which was chasing the rapidly fleeing Jap.

Being out in an open field without any shelter, we were completely unprotected and very vulnerable. As the planes disappeared from our view, everything became quiet again.

However, it was not for long. We heard planes again coming our way. This time we did not wait but ran as fast as we could to the camp and dived into the nearest shelter which happened to be an open trench.

While sitting in the trench with pounding hearts, we saw American planes flying overhead. What a beautiful sight that was. The huge silver birds continued to fly undisturbed by the anti-aircraft guns trained on them. The planes disappeared and nothing happened, to our immense relief.

Sometimes there were heavy daylight bombardments and we could hear the distinct sound of bombs dropping at a distance. More planes were engaged in these operations now and the target must have been close to our camp, but we didn't have a clue where. These raids lasted a long time, keeping us trembling with fear in the shelters for hours.

Once, after such an horrific bombardment, Bok'eh brought two napalm bombs, which he had found close to our camp. Some natives also brought some napalm bombs, which were still intact. But, despite our anxiety we still believed that our Allies knew we were in that camp.

More and more women were ordered to work in the sewing room which had to be greatly extended and was getting the appearance of a factory. Even the women working in the vegetable garden were recruited to work in the sewing room. All the sewing women had to work long hours, which produced a frantic, nerve-wracking atmosphere. The Japs had to get a lot of uniforms in a hurry. Why?

When someone working in the sewing room complained that they could not work such long hours on our grossly insufficient diet, Bok'eh flew into a rage. He roared like a lion. Who were the women to talk about food. He could very well let them eat rice only – nothing else.

However, when he saw the head of our kitchen, Mrs Den Hond some time later, he was shocked to see how thin she had become. She was a very hardworking and courageous lady, who told him that our diet was diabolical and deficient and that we were always feeling very, very hungry.

Then we all got better food, as far as possible in the circumstances. We got bread again on rare occasions, which was baked in the camp kitchen and for which we had to grind rice for flour.

We had forgotten what bread tasted like. The camp bread tasted delicious, even without butter. We also got some more vegetables but even so, our diet was still very poor and lacking in vitamins and protein.

28. 1944 – The Year of Death

Nineteen-forty-four continued its grim path at Kampili. A lot of people died and most of them were children. There was a total of 14 deaths in the year – 12 between October 29 and Christmas Day, nine of which were children under 10. Monsoon time is always gloomy but this period was worse than ever.

What touched me to the core of my heart was the death of two beautiful babies – Hansje and Tineke. Hansje was a gorgeous little boy with blond hair and blue eyes. He lived with his mother, who was in her 20s, in the barrack next to us. When he came to Kampili, Hansje was about six months old and his mother spread out a rug in a shaded spot and set her baby on it.

At that time he had little pink cheeks and he was a happy baby, always laughing and stretching out his little hands in pure delight. That was the picture I saw in June of 1943 when we were still trying to adapt ourselves to the impoverished living conditions we found ourselves in.

Hansje fell ill towards the end of this dreadful year with acute enteritis and died aged two on November 14. This beautiful little boy had to die because there were no medicines and proper food to treat him.

The same happened to the little poppet Tineke – or Robertina – who lived in our barrack close to us. She was a bit older than Hansje and died on December 21 from the same illness.

Tineke was like a beautiful doll, petite and with big brown eyes and dark, curly hair. The little girl's death had a profound effect on us all. How does one console a young mother with such a great and tragic loss? Tineke had a brother, who was a few years older, but Hansje was an only child, so his mother had lost everything. There were no husbands to share the grief. Sadly the husbands only heard after the war that their little ones had died.

I can never forget these two little children among the many who perished at Kampili late in 1944. Hansje, Tineke and the others had to die without the chance to grow up and without their mothers to hold their hands because of one dictator's greed for power. Where is the justice?

When my first little boy, Paul, was born with blond hair and blue eyes, pink cheeks and perfect health, the picture of Hansje came back to me.

Dysentery spread at an alarming rate. Bok'eh came back from Makassar one day with two Japanese doctors who had a large supply of some vaccine.

The vaccine was tried out on a small number of people first and I was one of the guinea pigs. We got a shot in an arm and my arm swelled up like a balloon and my temperature rose sky-high. I wasn't the only one with that reaction.

However, after the trial, everybody had to be vaccinated with the horrible stuff. We knew the Japs were petrified of contracting dysentery themselves and whatever they did was always with the view that it would be beneficial to them first. It made me wonder that if none of the diseases we were suffering from was contagious, would our Japanese masters have given a damn?

At the end of the year when the monsoon started, depression set in. This was obviously because of the weakening of our physical condition. In a short time six children under three had died and to cope with the increase in dysentery cases, a long flimsy bamboo barrack was built in great haste 15 minutes walk away from everybody and everything, where these sufferers were isolated.

Nobody was allowed to go there, only medical staff looking after the patients. At night they had no light in order not to attract 'enemy' (Allied) planes.

The latrines were open and a short distance from the barrack and the nurses had to walk in pitch-dark, no matter what kind of weather it was. The food for patients and staff had to be carried from the central kitchen to the barrack – an enormous job.

Flies were blamed for spreading the disease and Bok'eh ordered that every Saturday and Sunday, every person over 10 had to catch 200 flies this time. What a rotten job that was lumped on top of our normal job as well.

But still they died. Most of the children died of enteritis, a nutritional disorder and they died horrible, agonising, lonely deaths. Nothing could be done for the innocent little ones except hope the end would come mercifully quickly. For many, of course, it didn't and they had to spend days and long nights writhing in agony in their cots. The Japanese had a lot to answer for.

On account of the dysentery epidemic, we had to have spring cleaning sessions frequently. Now nurses were falling victim to the dreadful disease and others who had not contracted it had to work a lot harder. People looked exhausted and gaunt.

To cap it all off Allied bombardments were becoming more frequent and getting even closer to Kampili. More bomb trenches were dug but for Bok'eh, a bomb shelter was constructed deep underground close by his house.

He was acting more and more irrationally. His punishments were heavier and more frequent and women were forever being hauled out to stand in the sun in front of his house for hours or simply beaten with his stick, slapped in the face or copped a boxed ear.

Bok'eh would give orders and if these were not carried out immediately, punishment would result. He beat up one woman with his stick and when she fell to the ground he carried on the assault with vicious kicks to her head which she was attempting to protect.

Other women who had allegedly done something wrong would be given the dirtiest and heaviest jobs and the worst thing was that he always remembered people he had punished, so they were watched like a hawk.

Japs frequently visited our camp and they seemed to be very interested in some of the tiny houses which had been vacated by the occupants from Ambon, who had been housed in newly constructed bamboo barracks which formed complex C.

The purpose of the visitors' interest became clear some days later when baskets full of mica rocks arrived. Desks from our school in Makassar were delivered and placed in the empty little houses. The older teenagers were told to splice the mica. We had to sit two to a desk and were given an empty basket each, a supply of mica rocks and a wafer-thin knife-like thing, the point of which was as sharp as a razor blade.

For many hours a day we had to sit on the hard desk seats splicing the mica. A lot of very thin flakes could be spliced from one rock and we wondered what on earth these flakes would be used for.

At the end of the day we could not see straight. It was the most boring, stupefying job I'd ever done, and we'd been forced to do some mind-numbing things at Kampili.

The work played havoc with my poor head and I was plagued by more and more headaches of worsening severity. We had no lessons, just the mica splicing day in and day out and how I hated it.

Sitting on the hard wooden seat was very hard on my back as well. Worst of all, however, was the dreadful waste of time. It was like a mini version of old time prisoners having to break rocks but we had to be more delicate to produce these flakes of rock, for what use?

We learned in due course that we were actually working for the Japanese war machine. The mica we spliced was used to manufacture windows for their warplanes. Prisoners were not supposed to work for the production of enemy war materials. But who was going to stop these Japs? Nobody but the Japs themselves knew we were aiding their war production and they had not ratified the Geneva Convention, the gentlemanly agreement on the conduct of warring nations. Of course we didn't know that or anything about this Swiss convention which actually gave us, prisoners of war, some rights, so we went right on and split the mica.

29. From Bad to Worse

The tragedies of 1944 became 1945, the most disastrous time of the war years. Three more little children died in January and then on the 18th Jacoba Johanna Clasina Houwer died of dysentery, She was 16, the same age as me, and that really brought it home to me that I must be living on borrowed time, even though I was reasonably healthy.

The year started with torrential rain and it poured for days on end, drenching everything, including our most vital supply of firewood. This indispensable fuel shortage meant that our breakfast porridge was very late and we were lucky to get any more food that day.

Soon the firewood supply ran out and I was among a group of teenagers who were driven by truck to a small bush some distance from our camp. The Jap driver and his mate sat in the cab while we were bouncing up and down behind them in the open tray. They drove at high speed and when we arrived at the bush we were ordered to load the chopped firewood already lying there in a big heap. The wood was just tossed onto the tray and not secured.

Having put all the wood on the truck, we were ordered to sit on top of the loose logs and we had to cling to each other for dear life to avoid being flung off the truck which was being driven hell for leather back to the camp.

I shall never forget this event and it was a real miracle that we all arrived back safely. Of course we had to unload the wood as well and the result was wood splinters in my hands, which I suppose was a small price to pay for that hellish day.

Out of the blue, the commandant ordered that all the teenage girls had to get a new outfit consisting of a blouse and a skirt. The sewing room head told Bok'eh that the women had no time to sew these as they were snowed under with orders for Japanese uniforms.

So three older girls had to take care of this assignment. They got the materials and they made a pattern in four sizes and cut the outfits out of the materials. The mothers had to sew their daughters' garments.

Mamma and Leida sewed mine in their little bit of spare time and I became the proud owner of a navy blue skirt and pale orange blouse. There were no zips, so instead the skirt had two bands. One end of each band was sewn on the front and the other ends on the back of the skirt, crossing over at the back.

It felt really good to wear a new outfit, but we were only allowed to wear it when the commandant gave the order, which was when VIP Japs came and we had to line up and stand to attention and bow. The new clothes were really only meant to make a good impression, with Bok'eh doing his level best to be in the good books of his superiors, so he could stay in command at Kampili. Otherwise he would probably have had to go to the front to fight, which would have been a bit different. After all, American, Australian, New Zealand or British soldiers were a different kettle of fish from a group of defenseless women.

Some people actually believed he cared for us but Mamma, Leida and I, along with many others, would not have a bar of that. He really only cared for himself.

It didn't take long for the new outfit to lose its colour and its starch. The skirt soon faded to a dull grey colour and the blouse faded to a sickly, washed-out orange and the whole lot became limp and crumpled.

Kampili was a big camp and it was impossible to know everybody. Besides having to work hard and the little bit of school we managed to fit in, there was very little time for socialising.

Usually we were too tired at the end of the day to do anything else but to go to bed, hoping our precious sleep would not be interrupted by bombing that meant a rush to the shelters.

Tante Dora, Olga and the Salvation Army nurses were in barracks in complex A, right at the other end of the compound, so we had little contact with them.

In the tropics it grows dark very quickly. We had no electricity and we did not get any oil for our little individual lamps any more and because of the air raids we couldn't leave the barrack lamps burning either. What else was there to do, but drag our tired bodies to our shabby bunks.

Again Bok'eh did not seem to be himself. His moods were such that it was like treading on eggshells. You were forever waiting for him to start wielding that stick and praying you would not unwittingly be the victim.

One evening poor little Daantje, the commandant's assistant, really copped it. Bok'eh began by really abusing the poor youngster and then he took him outside the gate where he really laid into him with the stick and with vicious kicks. In the dead of night we could hear the poor little chap screaming in pain as the brute continued to flog him. Then Daantje was quiet but we could still hear the grunts of effort from the brute Bok'eh as the beating continued.

We thought Daantje must surely be dead but he survived. The next day he was in a terrible mess and walked very stiffly with widespread legs.

The reason for Daantje's thrashing was apparently because the young assistant had left a newspaper, printed in Malay, lying in a car and the newspaper had gone missing. The native driver of the car also received a horrific beating.

We supposed the newspaper contained good news for us and bad tidings for the Japanese. The result was that all sorts of optimistic rumours were circulating in the camp. Later on we heard that according to rumours, there was a report in that newspaper which said a high-ranking Japanese officer had been murdered by natives in Java or Celebes.

30. Mad Dogs

Misery was heaped upon misery in those early days of 1945. Dogs with rabies started wandering into the camp and this was the most scary of hazards. Three little children were bitten by a little rabid dog.

One child, Johannes Wesseling, aged seven, was bitten on his arm and even though the bite was burned out by a cigarette, he died on April 1. The other two were luckier – one was bitten on his little bottom and that bite had to be cut out, and the other received just a scratch. The mad dog was caught and beaten to death.

Dr Marseille was given a poison to kill the rabid dogs but everybody was petrified. A dog could wander into the camp at any time and we had absolutely no protection.

Rabies killed three people at Kampili. The second was a 20-year-old woman, Nelly Filet, on July 18. Two women were bitten during an air raid at night when the dogs attacked in total darkness. The women were treated in the commandant's bomb shelter and by the light in the shelter deep underground the women's bites were cut out and they survived.

Two weeks after Nelly Filet died, the camp's most heroic woman, Mrs C. F. M. Hoogeveen-de Hazewinkelman died of rabies. She was 33 and Mrs Hoogeveen had run to the aid of two women being worried by a rabid dog. With her bare hands she grabbed the animal by the throat and one of the women killed it with a cleaver. Unfortunately, Mrs Hoogeveen was bitten and when the symptoms appeared she withdrew from our community and isolated herself.

She warned everybody to stay away from her and alone, she fought for her life and died after horrendous suffering. We were all absolutely shattered and I will never forget this most courageous woman.

What really stunned us after her death was the indifference shown by the commandant. The pig of a man was angry at her action and as she lay dying from the convulsions and delirium, he refused her any aid, saying she should not have grabbed the dog. But had she not, the other two women and possibly more would have been bitten and probably died.

The commandant lashed out again at poor Daantje, flogging him so badly that his whole face was black and blue and very swollen. How this little, thin young man could endure such brutal treatment, I'll never know. It makes me feel sick when I think about it. Bok'eh , the fat brute, was much bigger and stronger than Daantje, who after all was his own compatriot and a harmless boy at that.

Bok'eh's violence made you very wary of him. I was scared of him and went out of my way not to be anywhere near him, he was so moody and unpredictable.

He was excellent at beating up innocent, defenceless people. Around this time he beat up a woman first on the face and then all over her body until she fell against a table. He ordered someone to fetch a bucket of water which he poured over the poor woman, who was by then vomiting blood. When the woman's daughter came to her mother's aid, he hit her with the back of his strong hand, alternately on her left and right cheek till her face was blood-red. The girl was screaming and mother and daughter were simply told to go away.

It's these really dreadful incidents that are ingrained in my mind and it was even more shocking because the poor woman had done nothing wrong. It appears he turned on her simply because he didn't like her. Getting beaten up really seemed to be a lottery.

31. The Grind Goes On

The commandant tried to ingratiate himself by initiating compulsory social evenings, of all things. At this stage the rate of victims suffering from beri beri, dysentery and other ailments like malaria and diphtheria caused by a lack of vitamins was horrifying, so the only attraction of these social evenings was the little bit of extra food that was promised.

Bok'eh seldom called a roll call these days, which was a relief because standing out under that cruel sun having to bow was a real pain. We didn't know why we were getting these little concessions but we heard later that the Japanese were having a bad time of it. The Japanese bosses in Makassar probably thought that if the Japs treated us well, then they would not be accused of ill-treating their prisoners. Of course it was too late by then.

Bok'eh was no animal lover. He got himself a monkey and the poor little creature had to sit on his bicycle handlebars tied to a rattling chain. Usually monkeys are good natured animals, like the lovely, intelligent one we had before the war, but the commandant incited his monkey so that it became vicious. He took great pleasure in letting the monkey jump on unsuspecting people.

This happened to Leida when she was concentrating on her work in the sewing room. Bok'eh sneaked up behind her and thought it was a great joke when Leida got the fright of her life. The monkey grimaced viciously at poor Leida.

The horrible brute used that animal to frighten women out of their wits but later the poor thing had to be destroyed because it had become too dangerous. Bok'eh had conditioned it to be violent and did a good job because it became vicious.

The commandant had a tennis court built. I was one of a group of teenagers engaged in pounding bricks to powder in rice mortars. The red powder was used to cover the deck of the court but it was awful, tiring work which caused sore arms and blisters on my hands.

When the tennis court was finished, the commandant played there frequently and usually got Dr Marseille to play opposite him. For the doctor, this was a pleasant change, because the poor man was forever being scolded and threatened with a beating. After all the hard work we could watch them play through the steel fence around the court.

Bok'eh was really looking after himself well. He had a Japanese bath installed behind the little women's hospital. The bath was connected to a large water drum and had a fireplace underneath. The fire had to be kept burning all the time so he could wallow in a steaming hot bath. Women had to stoke the fire and when one timidly remarked that this bath took an awful lot of water and firewood just for one person, he told them that they would be allowed to sit in the bath after he had finished. He could not understand why they refused.

Once after Bok'eh had finished his bath he walked around with his fat body wrapped in a towel and spotted Daantje, who was just returning to the camp.

When the little Jap got out of the truck which had delivered him, he was again beaten by the brute. He was beaten till he fell to the ground, then he was picked up and smashed down again. Nobody knew what Daantje was supposed to have done but whatever frustrations the commandant had was taken out on his poor assistant. It was really awful to see Daantje suffering like that with a multi-coloured swollen face as a result of the beatings. He never complained.

The women were given a break from the violence when Daantje was copping it and Bok'eh ordered that women who worked hard, like the sewing room workers, the pig farm attendants and the kitchen staff had to get better food. According to the commandant, ill people on special diets aimed at getting their strength back, did not need such food and it should go to people who 'really' deserved it. Heaven help those sick people.

Now there were almost daily heavy bombardments on Makassar. We could see fires raging in that direction and hear a resounding boom, boom, boom resounded which caused the ground to tremble and our barracks to shake. We spent many hours in our bomb shelters during the day as well as the night. But the the bombardments became more frequent and heavier during the night, so that we had to spend night after sleepless night in the shelters.

We learned that there was an airfield close to our camp. This airfield was also getting its share of treatment and we got very little sleep from having to go in and out of the shelters.

During the day, if there were no air raids we had to work and we became over-exhausted. There was still the threat of rabid dogs and on top of this we were pestered by hordes of mosquitoes and bugs.

Occasionally we got some meat but it was never enough. A small buffalo or a few goats, or even an occasional pig for 1700 meant we were always going to be hungry.

But the social evenings continued – even with dancing – though through being exhausted, hungry and having the minimum of clothes, how on earth could we enjoy ourselves? There was really nothing to enjoy anyway because things had only changed for the worse in the more than two years we had been there.

32. Praying for Leida

Suddenly Leida, who had not really had a day's illness since her bout of malaria, while all around her seemed to be stricken with something or other, got terribly sick with a mysterious infection in her head. She complained of a terrible pain behind her eyes and was carried to the little hospital where Mamma and I had also been patients.

Leida's condition worsened rapidly and she lapsed into a coma. Dr Goedbloed called Mamma and me to sit by Leida's side because she feared the worst and Lia was looked after by a kind person in the barrack.

My big sister lay motionless, her complexion deathly pale. Mamma and I were shattered and Mamma cried softly, while I tried to think what life would be like without Leida.

She and I were very close and I simply could not imagine life with her not in it. I looked up to her because, unlike me, she was not shy and always knew what to do and what to say.

The doctor and nurses were very understanding and as Mamma and I sat by Leida lying immobile on the bed, Dr Goedbloed told us to talk to her. I begged my sister to pull through.

After a week filled with great anxiety and sorrow for Mamma and me, Leida came out of the coma. I'll never forget that beautiful moment when she opened her big brown eyes. Very slowly she started the long and painful road back to recovery but for a long time she was very, very ill. It was a most worrying and uncertain time.

33. Shattered Beliefs

We saw many planes flying overhead these days and seemed almost to be permanently living in the bomb shelters. But, we had a strong belief that our Allies knew we were living there, even though it was extremely nerve-racking sitting there as targets. During the bombardments so close to us, the ground and barracks shook and shuddered as if there was a series of strong earthquakes.

One night when we were sitting in our bomb shelter we heard the droning sound of a plane flying over our camp. We could not see it as it flew at a high altitude, but we knew it was an American plane. Suddenly we heard a kind of whistling sound which came from some object which was hurtling down from the sky at great speed. There was a loud thud when the object hit the ground.

Then dead silence and the atmosphere was very tense. Nothing happened.

The object falling from the dark night sky appeared just to be an empty beer bottle, nonchalantly thrown from that lone, high-flying plane. The bottle came down with such a great force that its neck was embedded centimetres deep in the ground, pushing the soil up into its neck. It must have been an incredibly strong bottle to still be in one piece after having been thrown from such a height.

Rumours circulated that there was probably a message inside the bottle from our friends the Allies. We had pinned our hopes on it and what a great disappointment it was when it turned out to be an empty bottle. Part of the label was still on it but I can't remember what it was.

Then soon we were shaken out of our false belief that the Allies knew of our existence. The planes came over daily, dropping their lethal cargo at various locations dangerously close to our camp. At night we could see searchlights dashing through the dark sky and a small group of women had to take turns to operate the alarm bell. They had to be on duty day and night and these women were the most overworked in the camp. Some had to be admitted to our little hospital due to exhaustion.

It became clear now that we were smack in the middle of Japanese targets and some Japanese soldiers ventured inside our camp. They seemed to come from nowhere.

Every now and then we heard machine guns quite close to our camp. This was a very nervous time with everybody over-fatigued. But we had to keep going.

Leida was still in hospital but she was slowly getting better. The hospital had its own bomb shelters for the patients, although you can imagine that if we found it hard going, ill people must have found it even harder to cope.

The elaborate bomb shelter near Bok'eh's quarters was only for him to shelter in. Daantje and the little Jap who cut the uniforms which the women in the sewing room had to make, were not allowed to use it. Instead, these two Japs had to man two lookouts, one on the hospital roof and the other on top of the hill over the commandant's shelter. The commandant must have known what was going on outside our narrow, isolated world.

We heard the boom, boom, boom sound again, very close to us as planes flew overhead. We also heard machine guns, followed by white plumes just hanging in the sky like tufts of cotton wool and not moving at all. Sometimes we could even see the bombs dropping out of the planes, which made me feel very nervous and scared.

Occasionally we witnessed an attack in the air at close quarters between an

American and a Japanese plane. This was always accompanied by the sound of short, sharp, staccato gunfire.

Sometimes we happened to be working outside the camp when an air attack took place. Out in the open and no bomb shelters nearby, made us very vulnerable. We were also very frightened.

I remember one such air attack which took place very close to where we were working. A tall girl, several years older than me, ducked with me behind a low wall around an old dry well. The hair on the back of my neck stood straight up and I had goose-pimples all over. The other girl was a nervous wreck and I tried my best to calm her, which helped ease my fear.

The ack-ack-ack- suddenly stopped when the fight ended in the Jap's defeat and the plane plummeted to the ground and exploded on impact. A bright red ball of fire shot up followed by a black plume of dense smoke.

Just before his plane hit the ground the pilot ejected himself and sailed down to earth in his parachute. We could not see where he landed and the American plane disappeared very quickly before it could be shot down.

34. Droning Nightmare

There were so many air raids now that we were virtually bomb-shelter bound from 10pm until 7am, night after night.

Our Allies seemed to be carrying out a system of tiring out their enemy, as these were non-stop raids. At regular intervals we heard the droning sound of a plane followed by the dropping of bombs on different locations but now always very close to our camp.

Then one night, right on midnight, a bomb exploded so close to us that we thought a barrack had been hit. Immediately children started to cry and people panicked.

The explosion was very loud and sounded metallic and we were all very frightened and worried sick. Now, every time a bomber flew over we were all really tense and sweating, not knowing when and where the lethal object would be dropped. It was nerve-racking and exhausting and many people fell asleep in the shelters, seemingly oblivious to the danger they were in.

When the commandant's orders to go to the shelters immediately the alarm bell sounded were not carried out, he became panic-stricken. He yelled at the top of his uncouth Japanese voice to the people unable to walk fast enough and even went so far as to beat them with his stick to make them go faster.

Bok'eh tried to convince us that the Japanese had not wanted this war and blamed his country's hierarchy. Maybe he was right but we, isolated and subjugated, had no way of knowing. Whatever the truth, we should never have had to endure being at the mercy of these Japanese, although the irony of our present situation was that it was our Allies who were inflicting the damage on us.

But when Bok'eh had the audacity to say he felt sorry for us, we knew for certain he was lying. He was obviously scared for his own hide as he would have known at that time the Japanese were almost defeated.

The nightly air raids continued and our nerves were getting frayed. People were so exhausted that they giggled nervously like idiots, cried or quarreled. The commandant was very strict now and was getting even more neurotic as time went on.

If there was no air raid in the evening – a rare occurrence – Bok'eh insisted on everyone going to the 'club' to have a 'good time'. Mamma and I did not go as she wouldn't dream of leaving Lia alone in the barrack and Leida was still very ill in hospital. Besides, we had nothing to be joyful about, so how could we have a 'good time'. Women looked pale, which accentuated their always haggard and thin demeanor. They had no energy because they were all so exhausted.

Fortunately it did not rain during this period of air raids when we had to spend most nights in the shelters. The night sky was brilliant but when the moon and stars were hidden by cloud, it was quite eerie to hear the droning sound of planes flying overhead, not knowing if, when and where they were going to drop bombs.

There was a lot of activity in the air, day and night, and we heard the incessant sound of machine guns. We could see bombs dropping out of planes and there were always the terrible explosions when they hit the ground followed by the red glow of huge fires with their black, dense smoke.

35. They Were Our Friends

Our daily life was frequently disrupted but our marvellous teachers still tried to give us knowledge. For me, though, it was impossible to concentrate. I was physically and mentally exhausted like the rest but my health was deteriorating. I was becoming a nervous wreck with all the air raids.

I have to thank Mamma and her fantastic inner strength for keeping me sane and as I have said, I have nothing but praise for those dedicated teachers who, against all the odds and obstacles placed before them, continued to teach us. The teachers all had other jobs to do, some heavy manual tasks but they never complained or protested.

One day during a school session, we heard the almost ever-present droning of Allied planes. They came so suddenly that there was no time to sound the bell. We couldn't reach any shelter in time either, so we all dropped to the ground on the grassy plot in front of our little bamboo school.

Three huge planes appeared one after the other and flew so low they almost hit the roofs. We could clearly see the crews sitting in cockpits. It was unreal – they were our friends – but they gave no sign that they had seen us. It was unnerving. How come they did not see us lying there flat on the open ground.

Suddenly one of the planes shed a little boat-shaped silver-coloured object which came fluttering down like a leaf on the autumn wind. We heard a dull 'plop' and then there was dead silence. We got up quickly and ran as fast as we could to our barracks. Was it a bomb? But there was no explosion.

The commandant told us later that what had come from the plane was an empty fuel tank. He really made a great thing about it. The empty tank had come down right on top of a big mango tree in the kasbi (vege) garden. Under this same tree we girls and boys too, would take a rest (if permitted) while working in that garden or in the paddy field. It was sheer luck that those planes had not come a few hours earlier because in all likelihood some of us would have been sitting there. God had protected us.

After this incident it was crystal clear and now without a shadow of a doubt, that our friends the Allies did not know we were living there. It was a depressing and sobering thought.

The commandant became obsessed with us going to the shelters during air raids. We wondered why he particularly cared but I suppose any deaths would count dearly against him after the war, which he must have known was imminent.

But the big thing counting against Bok'eh's wishes was the fear of being bitten by a rabid dog, which were still a big and frightening problem. When it came down to it, we were more scared of being bitten and a lingering, horrifying death, than the likelihood of being killed by a bomb.

Bok'eh was having none of it. He beat the leader of barrack 11, the one next to us, to the ground because the people of her barrack stayed indoors, refusing to go to the shelters. He became paranoid and raged and raved if he saw anybody who had not gone into a shelter during the many bombardments.

He obviously knew what was going on and was very, very frightened. He often went to Makassar and sometimes high-ranking Japs turned up in Kampili and Bok'eh held meetings behind closed doors. Afterwards these Japs would leave in a great hurry. We never had to stand and greet these officers, which was the biggest sign that we were winning the war. But it was like living in a pressure-cooker, with the atmosphere extremely tense and everybody very frightened.

Then, sometime near the end of June 1945, we got a pleasant surprise. One night a plane dropped pamphlets and some had drifted down within our compound. They were orange and had a large photo of our Queen Wilhelmina stepping down from a plane, with Prins Bernhard, her son-in-law on her left and to her right the plane's pilot in uniform. Above the Queen's head was the Dutch coat of arms and at the feet of the trio was printed in huge letters in a ribbon-like band: "Seri Ratoe kembali ketanah Air" – "The Queen is back in the Fatherland."

A message was printed in Bahasa Indonesia saying that The Netherlands had risen again and Queen Wilhelmina was back on the throne. Then the message went on addressing the people of Indonesia, telling them not to be frightened because Indonesia would rise again.

The commandant was the last person to know about these pamphlets, which were obviously a great source of inspiration for us when we were desperately in need of one. When he found out he ordered them to be handed in and Daantje had to burn them. Naturally, not all were handed in.

Our first good news that was real, not part of a rumour mill and not an interpretation of one of Bok'eh's moods. Our dear little country had been liberated.

But the war was far from over for us. Mamma and I were still very worried about Leida, who was still quite ill in hospital. The only thing I could do was pray to God to make her better.

In July the bombardments executed by the Americans were dreadful. Most of the time the airfield close to us was their target. They pounded it and the ground shuddered. Our flimsy barracks swayed dangerously but held out. We didn't expect them to last because they were taking plenty of punishment from the bombing so close to us.

Then the weather changed. It rained and it rained and the nights were damp and chilly and all the shelters, whether open or closed, were sopping wet. We had to go into these dank places as soon as the alarm sounded under the threat of a beating.

Going in and out of the wet shelters took its toll. There were many sick people, especially children and our little, thin Lia suffered a lot from asthma.

There were a lot of Japanese soldiers stationed nearby. We had seen them on bikes with packs on their backs pedalling God only knows where. We also saw them walking along the road in front of our compound and at night we could hear them sing.

The commandant got another animal, a horse. Without a saddle he sat on the horse and galloped around the compound at high speed like a madman digging his heels into the poor horse for more speed.

36. The Inferno

Mercifully we were given a break from air raids for a while giving us the chance to sleep in our hard, uncomfortable beds. But who cared. It was better than trying to sleep in those shelters.

But this proved to be the lull before the storm when all hell broke loose and our world, on tenterhooks as it was, was completely shattered.

It was Tuesday, July 17, more than two months since Europe had celebrated victory over Germany. In the morning everything was as normal with people at work. About midday planes were heard and the alarm sounded and I dived into the nearest bomb shelter. Soon the all clear was given and I ran to our barrack at the same time Mamma arrived from the sewing room.

Leida was still in hospital and as far as Mamma and I knew, Lia was one of a small group of children her age getting some schooling. We didn't know exactly where they were but they would be safe in a shelter and the teacher would look after them.

The hand-operated alarm bell sounded again, this time with greater urgency. Something was terribly wrong that the alarm sounded so loud and furiously.

Mamma and I hurried to our open shelter. The planes were now heading in our direction and there were many of them. They were dropping things that looked like parcels and when they'd dropped these parcels the planes veered away. The parcels were napalm.

Then someone came running to us, screaming that they were bombing our camp. "They've hit the pig farm and A and C complexes". She was in great shock and absolutely hysterical. More terrified people were running around, screaming their heads off.

The pig farm, barracks in A and C complexes and some of the little houses in which the people from Ambon were originally housed were burning fiercely. We heard bamboo exploding and saw a red glow from the huge fires. Thick black smoke was rising into the sky. An acrid smell drifted our way affecting our throats and breathing.

I felt the hair on my neck stand up and I had goose pimples all over. I was paralysed with fear. A proper stampede then occurred, with people running to the gate, their bare feet pounding the ground. They flew out the gate, raced over the bridge and across the road into the little ravine. They were joined by the few camp cows, because their shed was also burning fiercely, having had a direct hit.

The commandant was beside himself yelling to some people who tried to save whatever they could of their meagre possessions to leave them and get the hell out of the camp.

The planes returned. Large silvery machines with big bulging bellies like grotesque pregnant birds. The alarm bell sounded with even greater urgency, if that was possible, although this was hardly needed with everyone aware of the planes and the danger. Again the planes dropped many napalm bombs and more buildings were hit and more fires started. There was complete pandemonium.

Mamma and I did not run with the others but stayed by our barrack. After the all-clear we left the shelter and walked to our barrack which was still undamaged and Mamma told me to go to the big, beautiful tree we always admired from our little windows.

She wanted to rescue as much as she could and I had to stay there under the tree while she went inside the barrack to fetch our few possessions. Mamma said: "I won't be long. Just wait there. I'll get our things and bring them out there. Don't follow me."

So I did as I was told and stood waiting under that beautiful, living tree. I was still numb with shock and petrified. I saw Mamma disappear into our barrack through one of the doorless openings. There was nobody else around and it was eerie as most of the other camp buildings were burning fiercely. I could see the flames and smoke and feel the awful heat.

Mamma had only been inside our barrack for a little while when I saw to my horror that our block had also caught fire. The hip of the palm leaf roof was well alight and all of a sudden huge tongues of fire, fanning out, were rushing along the top of the length of our barrack roof and in no time the whole roof was ablaze. There was still no sign of Mamma.

I became hysterical and started to scream in a high-pitched note and continued screaming without even knowing what I was doing. Suddenly I felt a sharp hard slap across my cheek and I stopped screaming immediately. I rubbed my sore cheek and then I came to and saw Mrs Lucas, the tall, gaunt woman the flat of whose hand had delivered the blow. She used to live in the barrack next to us and she was a really nice person.

When she heard my story she comforted me and when she had calmed me down, she left because she was sure that Mamma would be coming soon. She also had children, so she wasn't staying a minute longer in the area of the inferno.

I was convinced I would lose Mamma, who would be burned beyond recognition. She was the only one I had left at that particular time, as I did not know where Leida and Lia were or whether they were still alive. All I knew was that Mamma was inside that burning barrack. I felt so alone and I couldn't imagine being left in that hell-hole.

At the same time as the planes were bombing our camp, many Japanese soldiers appeared from nowhere and fired at the big planes flying overhead. The planes fired back, making the situation even more perilous. I was in the middle of the crossfire with bullets flying all around me. This was the most terrifying moment in my life but when the planes veered away the guns went silent.

After what seemed an eternity, Mamma emerged from our burning barrack, the frame and walls of which were now on fire. Mamma was carrying our only suitcase in one hand, in which she had packed our miserable few possessions and in her other hand she was clutching her bulging handbag and two children's raincoats.

Fires were raging all around us and the furious flames devoured everything. Barracks, loos and everything else burned fiercely and crackled loudly. Bamboo exploded and was catapulted into the air. Rags of soot were whirling around in the intense heat, which was unbearable. The air was acrid and smoke-filled and breathing was becoming difficult and my eyes and my throat were sore.

I begged Mamma by screaming at her to leave immediately and get out of the danger. I was trembling all over. Mamma put the suitcase under the tree, which still looked so majestic and tranquil next to the raging inferno. She kept the handbag under her arm and carried the raincoats with her. "We'll have to go through the barbed wire fence," she said. This was now the only way out for us because by the main gate fire was engulfing everything.

We had just managed to crawl through the barbed wire fence when those dreadful huge planes returned. Mamma and I fell face down in the gutter which ran parallel to the fence and I pulled the two children's raincoats over my head and shoulders and prayed and prayed and prayed, like I had never prayed before. I held on to Mamma's legs in front of my face and I lifted the tip of the coat to see what was happening.

The planes made a wide swoop and dived very low as they approached. Oh, my dear God. The big silver planes opened their bellies and napalm bombs rained down like arrows shot from many bows. There were many planes. In a terrifying instant I realised that Mamma and I would be killed. We would be hit by napalm bombs and killed very slowly as the gauze inside them burst into flame on impact.

I heard thuds all around us, expecting one of those bombs to land on me and Mamma at any second. And then I heard the planes fly away and I took the coat off my head to have a look and saw that one of the napalm bombs had missed one of my legs by inches. The bomb was stuck in the soft ground, so the napalm on the gauze did not get a chance to burst into flame.

The heat of the burning camp was horrendous and the exploding bamboo sounded like a fierce, private battle being fought. My legs were numb and the rest of me was shaking like a leaf. Our barrack, number 12 in complex B, that flimsy familiar building which had been our home for years, burned fiercely and then collapsed into a heap of red glowing hot ash.

The planes had gone and the crews which manned the huge planes would have thought they had done a good job, unaware of the havoc and utter misery they had inflicted on us.

But how were they to know? The horrible Japanese had never put a red cross sign on our camp and from the air our camp must have looked like any other military camp. The bombers had done a thorough job. Everything burned to the ground and there was only complete destruction left.

We were now on the outside of the barbed wire fence but we were still prisoners.

Mamma and I crawled out of the gutter and everywhere the fires were still burning fiercely. The air was acrid and suffocating and the place gave me the creeps. Mamma and I made our way along the outside of the fence, over the filthy canal and across the road where, in a little densely-treed valley, we found all the camp people huddled together. Thank God, Leida and Lia were there too. Leida had gone with the other hospital patients to the bushy valley and Lia was taken there with a group of children.

All around this group of defeated women and children who were very frightened and feeling particularly miserable, stood Japanese soldiers with guns guarding them. Everybody was quiet and numb with fear and I was still in great shock.

I can't remember how long we stayed in that little raving with the Japs and their guns but after a time the sound of crackling fires died as the flames ran out of material to devour.

But at last, after what seemed an eternity, we were allowed to go back to the camp across the road. What a sad, eerie scene awaited us. All the bamboo buildings were reduced to big heaps of hot ash. Where we once lived was only hot ash. We had lost our home and miserable as it was, it was the only home we had. Where would we all go now?

The wells stood naked and the water was full of soot and all that was left of our loos were the holes in the ground and the little raised steps on either side of the loo holes.

People started to poke around in the ashes in the hope of retrieving some things which the flames had missed. Mamma found the cast-iron rice cooker with the lid, which we had used as a chamber pot. We couldn't go too close to the ash as it was too hot and we were all mostly barefoot.

We went back to our big beautiful tree where Mamma had left the suitcase with our few possessions. Mamma hurried up to the suitcase but when she touched the lid, it collapsed into a heap of ash. The tree and the suitcase had suffered a direct hit and the resulting fire had destroyed all we owned and our beautiful tree was very badly damaged. To think that tree was wrecked just minutes after I had stood under it waiting for Mamma.

That big leather handbag that went everywhere with Mamma, even to bed, had survived the inferno. It had everything that was precious to us in it and people would laugh at Mamma and say: "There goes Lous with her big bag," and Mamma would reply: "You can laugh but it won't stop me taking my bag wherever I go."

She was as good as her word, even during the endless hours spent in the bomb shelters, that bag would stay under her arm. At all her jobs – the hospital laundry and the sewing room – that bag was there.

The old leather handbag made it to our liberation and beyond but finally gave up the ghost. It had done a sterling job in holding all the important documents, wedding rings and watches. Strangely enough, though, and unusually for Mamma, she had forgotten to take our birth certificates and we all had the devil of a job getting them when we needed them.

37. Puppets of Propaganda

Poor Mamma had taken a great risk in saving the small suitcase with our worldly possessions but it had been in vain. We had lost everything except the clothes we wore, the rice cooker, two children's raincoats and the big leather handbag with its contents.

But we didn't have much time to worry about our loss because we were ordered to assemble on the field by the commandant's tennis court.

Japanese reporters had arrived carrying big cameras. We were ordered to sit together, a dirty, dishevelled, shabby lot of women and their children. While the journalists were getting their cameras ready, word went round that one of the women would give the order to turn around and put our bottoms up to the cameras. At the very right moment, just as the Japs were about to click the shutters, our group, as one, turned around and put our backsides up in the air facing the cameras. Despite our misery, we had a good laugh. I cannot remember what happened after that but I think the Japanese managed to get some decent shots of us surrounded by heaps of ash.

We learned that they were taking these films back to Japan, presumably to show people at home how our friends the Allies had treated us by dropping bombs and destroying everything. Of course they would not be telling the people at home that we were sitting ducks. They would also not tell them that our camp was next to a Japanese military base and that they had not identified our camp as being a prisoner of war base housing 1700 women and children.

All the bamboo buildings had been razed and the stone buildings were badly damaged. It was all so terrible that it makes me wonder how we coped, not only physically but also psychologically and emotionally.

There were seven people killed, all hit during the first bombardment. One woman, Mrs Dahler-Voerman, aged 23, was hit by a napalm bomb which went through her thigh and nailed her to the ground. She was taken to Makassar and her leg was amputated but she died four days after the attack on July 21.

Four other victims died after indescribable suffering, including two little girls who died of extensive napalm burns. The other two deaths were a woman, Mrs H.W. van Sandick-Coldenhof, who had horrific burns and was treated next to Leida in the hospital, and a teenage boy. Mrs van Sandick was only 31. Leida said she had talked constantly about dying and going to be with Jan, her husband. We learned later that Mrs Sandick-Coldenhof had been forced to witness the beheading of her husband somewhere in the interior of Celebes, so having that nightmare constantly with her during her hours of agony before she died three days later must have been a terrible burden, although in a strange way it was also something of a comfort as they were to meet again. Such faith was always very sobering to us on the outside, still very much alive – in body at least.

There was simply nothing which could have saved these unfortunate people and it was a miracle that not more people were killed.

The pig farm, complexes A and C and some of the little houses where the Ambon people had lived, were destroyed during the first bombardment. The women working at the pig farm had little time to seek shelter and the piggery burned down in no time, killing most of the pigs.

The sudden bombardment had given the women no time to rescue the pigs and they were lucky to get away in time themselves. There were some survivors among the pigs but these poor animals had hideous burns on their bodies and their skin was hanging down in tatters. They had virtually been roasted alive.

Some people killed them to put them out of their misery and others feasted greedily on the roasted pig meat, risking illness because their stomachs were not used to such rich food after having lived for such a long time on a poor diet of rice and the odd vegetable.

38. Boskamp

The Japs must have expected the destruction of Kampili because they had an emergency camp ready for us. We had to walk some distance over narrow paddy field dykes to our new accommodation.

This camp was really the limit. It was the most primitive, unhealthy and depressing place, consisting of a group of very small bamboo hovels built in the bush under huge trees. The trees had large roots which spread from the trunks out in a cartwheel fashion right around the tree. Part of the roots were above ground and we had to be careful not to trip over them or stub our toes. The tree canopies were dense and shut out the sunlight. We called this camp Boskamp (Bush Camp).

The hovels were very primitive. They were built of bamboo on bamboo poles with a rough ladder to climb up on and into the one bare room without door or window. There were nowhere near enough of these huts to house all of us, so about 30 of us were packed in them like sardines. We had to sleep on our sides. Wecould not turn over without disturbing our neighbours on both sides.

As there were no latrines at this camp we had to go into the bush and use leaves as loo paper.

Later, a big pit was dug and covered with bamboo slats. A flimsy low wall was erected around this pit and one had to squat over an opening between the slats. That was so degrading and we had no privacy at all.

There was no water there either, so we had to carry it from the old camp. There was always a long queue of women navigating the narrow dykes in both directions, carrying food and water from Kampili to the dreadful Boskamp.

Kampili's central kitchen survived the inferno and a group of women stayed there to cook our meals. The bathroom walls had been destroyed and the wells were still there with sooty water. But we needed that water, so we carried it to the Boskamp to have a wash somewhere in the bush behind a big tree.

There were no bomb shelters at Boskamp either, so in the event of an air raid, we had to lie between the enormous roots of the trees. Nobody was allowed to run in the new camp and we had to lie very still so as not to be seen by 'enemy' planes – our Allies.

In this dreadful, unhealthy and hazardous environment, dysentery spread like wildfire. Sanitation, hygiene and all the things needed for safe living were non-existent.

Morale was at its lowest point and many people became really depressed. I was suffering from deep shock – shell shock I suppose.

After being in Boskamp for two days we heard that horrible, ominous drone of aircraft again. We hurried to the giant trees without making any noise and lay down between the huge roots. We had to lie dead-still because any movement, however slight, could attract the attention of the planes' crew.

The planes were returning to finish their job of destruction at Kampili. Their targets were what was still standing after the carnage inflicted two days before. Still undamaged were a number of stone buildings which had escaped the inferno.

This time they dropped the impact bombs, leaving huge craters and destroying everything in and around the area. The explosions were horrific and every time a bomb exploded the earth shook violently. The loud bangs were very hard on our eardrums and the only thing we could do was put our fingers in our ears. We also had to put something between our teeth, such as a piece of erasing rubber, if you were lucky enough to have some. Otherwise we had to stuff something else between our teeth to prevent them from cracking.

This time I went into even deeper shock. I could hardly breathe and my face was so swollen I could hardly look out of my eyes. After the all-clear, Mamma called the doctor. Dr Goedbloed came immediately and examined me there and then lying under a giant tree. She said I was not to be moved and she would come back later. I had to lie very still.

I lay there oblivious to people's activities. I can't remember how long I lay there under that tree, which shaded me from the blazing sun and made me invisible from the air. I remember very little of that episode but Mamma was very worried. Dr Goedbloed came back and my condition had improved somewhat and I was allowed to get up but take things easy.

The damage done by that second bombardment at Kampili was disastrous. There was not much left now except ruins. The little stone bungalows, the central kitchen and the commandant's house and office were very badly damaged. Both little hospitals, the women's and the children's, were reduced to pitiful crumbling ruins and where the bombs had hit there were deep craters. The food storage shed was completely ruined and the commandant's bathroom had collected a direct hit. No more hot steam baths for Bok'eh.

The Japanese promised the camp would be rebuilt.

The bombing was by no means over and because our camp was blasted off the face of the earth, the Allies now concentrated on the air base and the Japanese military base nearby, which they obviously hadn't done a very good job of destroying in their earlier raids. We could only hope and pray that Boskamp had not been seen.

An air raid could happen at any time and you could be anywhere. You could be walking between Kampili and Boskamp – 10 to 15 minutes away – fetching water or carrying food. There would be no time to reach a shelter, so the only thing you could do was to fall flat and face down under a shrub and lie absolutely still while praying all the time they were not going to drop any more bombs.

Lack of sanitation became an enormous health hazard. Because there was only one toilet pit for all of us, many people still used the bush and leaves. The stench was terrible and so were the flies, so more pits had to be dug and sprinkled with lime and kerosene needed to be poured into them.

Another health hazard were the rotting carcasses of the dead pigs. Some teenage boys were ordered to bury them in deep pits and they did this with no masks, gloves or footwear.

39. Execution Day

People still poked around in the ash of Kampili but not everyone handed in the things which did not belong to them and this created much unpleasantness.

Fortunately Leida was just well enough by now to stay with us. During her stay in hospital she had worn a pretty nightie Mamma had kept from when we left Makassar three years ago. She was wearing the nightie on the night of the inferno and later, after Leida had discarded it for her shapeless hansop when she got out of the hospital, Mamma spotted the nightie hanging on the outside of one of the huts and she resolutely walked up and took it. She was walking back to our hut when a woman rushed outside and abused Mamma, who calmly told her the nightie belonged to Leida and that was the end of it. That nightie, the clothes we were wearing the day of the inferno and the two children's raincoats were the only garments we had left.

Rabid dogs were still a threat and a big worry, especially during the night when it was pitch black and there was no lighting anywhere.

And talking about mad dogs, the commandant was completely off his rocker and very dangerous. He took to carrying a sword and one day he decided he was going to use it to execute Mrs Valderpoort, the leader of the Ambon group of people, who apparently had been seen outside the zone limits of Boskamp.

Mrs Valderpoort was a very respectable women, very religious and very just. First the mad Bok'eh ordered her into his office, or what was left of it, and then he ordered her to stand to attention outside his office in the blazing sun. He was obviously determined to carry out the beheading and even had the priest measure her for the size of the coffin. He ordered some natives to dig a grave.

Mrs Joustra, our leader, tried to reason with the raving Jap and talk him out of this barbaric plan. At first she did not seem to have any luck and he shouted at her that he would take his victim outside the camp so nobody would have to witness the execution.

For some time it was a very dangerous and tense situation and whatever happened to change his mind I don't know but in the end Mrs Valderpoort's life was saved. What she must have gone through is indescribable and her faith in God must have kept her sane. We all admired her incredibly for the way she carried herself during the incident but it only made us hate and fear the commandant more than ever.

Our misery never seemed to end. It started to rain and it rained non-stop for days on end. Our roof leaked like a sieve and all we had to cover us were the two raincoats. There was mud everywhere and we were wet all the time because whatever we did we had to go out in the rain. We had no place to shelter except the leaking hovel.

Boskamp had to be guarded during the night and we had to take turns in walking shifts around the camp, two at a time. Leida had made an amazing recovery by then, so she and I teamed up and when our turn came up the hell-hole Boskamp was guarded by two teenage girls.

We were barefooted, we stumbled over and stubbed our toes on the tree roots. To find our way in the pitch dark we were given a tiny light which consisted of a very small wick floating in a bit of coconut oil in a little tin. We also carried a stick in case we encountered a rabid dog but fortunately we never did.

But the possibility still makes me shudder. The poor people who were bitten died a horrible death. God must have protected us from all those dangers we experienced during our captivity.

One night during our watch, while we were carefully and slowly negotiating the huge roots and our figures threw grotesque spooky shadows on the path beneath the trees, we got a terrible shock. When we slowly approached a corner we saw a dark shape wrapped up in what looked like some cloth. We stopped, scared stiff and held our miserable light a little closer to the figure.

The thing suddenly came to life and a face suddenly appeared above the cloth and a voice said: "Djangan takut. Saya pendjaga." ("Don't be afraid, I'm a guard.") Then the man withdrew within his cloth cocoon again. The cloth was a sarong and we noticed then that he was sitting on a chair. He had a chair, even if it was an old one while we didn't have one chair or a stool for the lot of us.

Who had appointed that man and if he was getting paid for sitting there in one corner, we never knew. There was only one such guard and the mosquitoes couldn't get to him but Leida and I were just about eaten alive. We were lucky we didn't catch malaria.

There were still air raids but now that our camp had been completely destroyed, they concentrated on Makassar and the nearby airfield.

One day I happened to be in Kampili when the alarm went off. The nearest shelter was a closed one which was still intact. There were more people running to that shelter and I waited until they were all inside before I went in. This was to ensure I was near the exit. Sitting next to me was a nun who was praying and this gave me some courage to get over my acute claustrophobia.

I was really in a mess at that time after the shell-shock attack. Psychologically and emotionally I was shot, although I tried not to let on to anybody and nobody actually knew, not even Mamma, how desperately frightened I was. It wasn't so much the air raids but having to go into a closed shelter, as well as the fear of being bitten by a rabid dog.

This fear would not leave me and it pestered me day and night. It would not leave me and I had no peace because of it. I also suffered appallingly from the shocking conditions at Boskamp – the threat of rabid dogs, the exhausting job of having to carry water and food from Kampili, the stench from the sewer pits, as well as the flies, huge rats, mosquitoes and bugs – caused me great stress.

Of course there was no such thing as counselling but Mamma had an inner strength and great courage that I could rely on and it was due to her that I could just cope.

The food storehouse in Makassar had been destroyed, so they told us, so we had to eat burned rice. People suffered indigestion as a result.

40. Peace at Last

With conditions becoming almost impossible to bear and morale at its nadir, the air raids suddenly stopped. Everything went very quiet. No planes were heard or seen, something that was beyond belief after the pounding our nerves had taken over the past year or more. It was almost eerie and unreal and we had no idea why.

Then, on August 16, what we had longed for all those years really happened. A message was written on the board nailed to one of the huge trees near the entrance of Boskamp telling us to assemble on the grassy area called the cow meadow. Great excitement rippled through the camp and everybody ran, forgetting that it was prohibited to run, to the place of assembly. In Boskamp under the giant trees, the feet pounding the ground sounded like a herd of elephants stampeding in the forest.

We were full of expectation. The daily bombing raids had ceased days before, which perhaps dared us to think today's announcement was to tell us the war was over. A chair from the commandant's ruined quarters was placed in the middle of the meadow. The commandant was to make an important announcement.

He had to climb onto the chair but the brute who was never short of a word during our interminable confinement under his command, couldn't utter a single word. Instead he asked Mrs Joustra, our leader who had been informed of the good news, to tell the excited throng. Bok'eh just disappeared.

Mrs Joustra climbed onto the chair and looking into the sea of pale, thin, expectant faces, she told us with a trembling voice and holding back the tears, that the Japanese had capitulated on August 15, the day before. Yes, yes, yes ... the war was over.

But while the war was over, it was just the beginning of the end of our confinement. The authorities in Makassar told us through Mrs Joustra that the military hospital there would be vacated so the seriously ill patients from Boskamp and the civilian men's camp at Pare Pare and the prisoner of war camp at Makassar could be taken there and nursed back to health. The rest of us had to wait until houses in Makassar were made ready to accommodate us. We were also strongly advised not to communicate with the natives. They told us this was in our own interests but did not tell us the reason. We suspect the Japanese wanted to keep the natives ignorant of the Allied victory for as long as possible.

After hearing the wonderful news, people were at first stunned. Many simply could not believe it ... they'd known hardship and war for so long. But when they at last realised that it wasn't some mean trick, there was jubilation. Peace at last – how absolutely wonderful.

People cheered, shouted, danced and hugged each other and cried. Then, after the initial euphoria, the mood became subdued as we all wondered about loved ones who weren't with us – husbands and sons.

We were relieved that at last there was peace in the world and now we did not have to fear those awful air raids and machine-gun fires any more. The war was over, even though we were not really free yet.

We were still in that hell-hole of a camp. There were a lot of dysentery patients and there were more deaths too – two middle-aged women died of dysentery in the first two weeks after peace was declared – very tragic and very, very depressing.

41. Lingering On

Although the war was over there was little change in our conditions. Only a small group of women who cared for the sick and those who cooked our meals, were accommodated at the old camp.

Our food had not improved either. Rather, it had deteriorated as the heavy task of carrying it from the kitchen in Kampili to Boskamp was becoming too great a burden. How long would we have to live like this? Nothing was happening. We should have been taken out of this dump and been given proper housing, food and clothes. Many were suffering a variety of health problems getting over exhaustion and combating the poor diet and shocking sanitary conditions.

Mrs E.A. Logeman-Hartelust, a 54-year-old woman who lived with us in barrack 12 at Kampili, fell ill with dysentery and died on August 29. How incredibly sad that she had endured those awful years, only to die so close to liberation. She was such a nice lady and I cannot forget her.

Natives were building new bamboo barracks at Kampili, the same as the old ones and on the same sites where they had been reduced to ash. They were very slow workers and we were wondering if we would be able to move into them before we could return to Makassar.

Bok'eh was still in charge, although he had gone to live outside the camp. He still wanted to be boss and still we had to ask him permission for this and that. Didn't we beat the Imperial Japanese Army? It was a crazy situation really but there was nobody else until the arrival of the Dutch or another Allied power.

Out of nowhere Bok'eh seemed to conjure up things such as a basin for us all. All those awful years we did not get anything and now were getting things that were always essential. Maybe the Japs wanted to make a good impression.

The brute Bok'eh still tried to intimidate us. He had the habit of sharpening his sword and trying to frighten women by flashing the glinting sword in front of them. Seeing the women become very nervous, he stood close in front of them as they trembled, enjoying the scene with a sadistic grin on his face.

A large black cloth with the letters P.W. in white had been spread out on the paddock where we had assembled to hear the wonderful news of the end of the war. According to Bok'eh, this had been ordered by the Allied powers. If the Japanese had put the same sign up as soon as we moved into Kampili, our Allies would not have bombed us out. We could never forgive that.

On August 31, we celebrated Queen Wilhelmina's birthday with a party organised by the leaders. We got very nice sweets, made by natives, a small amount of sugar and a very good meal. Then all sorts of games were organised with little prizes. I don't know where all the stuff came from. We had almost forgotten what pencils, soap, notebooks, handkerchiefs and talcum powder looked like. Some tables and chairs were brought in and what a treat it was to sit on a proper chair.

There was a large white screen with Queen Wilhelmina's portrait on it and surrounded by flowers and flags. Seeing the Dutch red, white and blue flag gave me goose pimples.

I never found out who gave all the things or where they came from but it is possible the Japs had ordered the natives to produce them. There were also church services. In the morning there was high mass and in the afternoon the Protestant service.

Then it was September and still no news and no change in our conditions and we were back on a meagre diet again.

Three barracks were completed and some lucky people could move from Boskamp to the new Kampili but unfortunately, we were not among them.

Some very sick people were transported to hospitals in Makassar. Some could not walk. Thank God Leida had recovered and could stay with us.

42. The Lists

We had not seen Pappa since that tearful farewell in Makassar when we drove off in Tante Dora's car towards Malino in January 1942. That was three-and-a-half years of not knowing where he was and what had become of him, apart from the brief report from the Indonesian man who risked his life coming to Malino to report to us that Pappa was a prisoner of war but that he appeared fit and healthy.

So when the lists of names of all the menfolk belonging to the women and children at Boskamp and Kampili came in and were pinned to the notice board on the big tree at the entrance to Boskamp, everything was dropped and there was a big rush to see what list your particular loved ones appeared on.

One list had all the names of the deceased men of Makassar and Pare Pare, the second had the names of all the POWs of Makassar who had been transported to Java, Japan and Burma, while the third list named the survivors of the POW camp at Makassar and the civil men's camp at Pare Pare.

Mamma asked Leida and me to look for Pappa's name. My legs almost gave way as I approached the first list – the dead – and I heard Leida say beside me: "Pappa's name is not on this one." The relief was fantastic – he was alive.

We moved to the second one and yes, Pappa had been moved to Java. We raced back to Mamma and told her the good news and she cried happy tears.

But we were almost ashamed to be happy. Many men would never come back. Lily, our barrack crier who had received that horrific beating from Bok'eh the previous year, had lost her husband in the POW camp in Makassar. The husband of Lies, our immediate neighbour in barrack 12, had been killed in action fighting for our country, so that meant little Marianne and Wietse were fatherless. There were many others and it was devastating to see the names of all those men who had died in circumstances we could not begin to imagine.

While we had suffered terribly during our time in captivity, it would have been nothing compared with the men, whom we now know were treated so brutally by their Japanese captors. That more didn't die was testimony to the hardiness of the Allied menfolk.

43. A Plane Comes in Peace

One morning early in September we heard the sound of a plane. At first it brought back horrible memories of all those planes we used to hear and the sound was the cue to rush for the bomb shelters. That was during the war though and now we were at peace.

The plane came closer and closer and everybody ran out into the open and there were happy cries when it was realised it was a Dutch plane. The small plane had the red, white and blue painted on its side. It was one of ours and what a wonderful sight it was as it flew three times over Boskamp almost brushing the treetops. People were ecstatic and they shouted joyfully and waved and danced. Tears of joy flowed freely but not all were jubilant as there were others, particularly children, who were still very scared of planes.

Some orange coloured pieces of paper fluttered down from the plane. On these was printed in Dutch that a white cross, the measurements of which were given, had to be placed on the ground in an open space. The three men in the plane promised to come back the following day to drop food. They also advised us that it would be wise to appoint a group of people who would be responsible for collecting and distributing the dropped food supplies and that we had to stay a great distance away from the white cross when the drop was taking place in order to avoid accidents.

The Dutch plane's visit was a great event and it gave plenty of people the chance to be very emotional. The plane had frightened me at first, especially when I couldn't at first see the plane. But it was wonderful to see the red, white and blue painted on the side.

The crew's instructions were carried out and a big cross was laid out on a large empty space of land. As promised they came back the next day and dropped a number of small, dark green army drums. They flew so low that we could clearly see the men in the plane and saw them push the drums out of the plane's door.

It was a baking hot day and we had not had any rain for some time, so the ground was rock hard. On impact, the drum lids came off and the contents spilled out all over the ground. There, before our eyes spread out on the dirty ground, were raisins, packets of egg powder, chocolate and other food items we had not seen for almost four years.

When the drop was completed and the plane disappeared over the horizon, we were ordered by the appointed collectors to pick up all the raisins, one by one, the packets of egg power and all the other goodies except the chocolate and hand them in. They supervised us to make sure nobody was cheating and having a sly snack on the luxurious food items.

As it came down, the chocolate melted in the hot sun and dripped on the soil and dry yellow blades of grass. So immediately after the other food had been handed in, Leida and I and plenty of children, crawled around on all fours or slid along on our stomachs licking off the heavenly chocolate. What a delight. After all those years we had forgotten what chocolate tasted like.

The sun was beating down but that didn't worry us as we crawled, shuffled, slid and licked and licked till there was not a melted drop left. It didn't matter that much of it had dirt stuck on it – it still tasted delicious.

All the food that was collected was distributed equally and we were in heaven being able to eat that lovely food after having lived so long on an incredibly poor, dull diet.

We never saw that plane with the Dutch tri-colour on its side and the three Dutch crew again and much later we heard they had died when they flew into a mountain.

Some days after the Dutch plane's drop, an American plane flew over. We watched as long containers hanging on parachutes slowly floated down to the camp. The cylinder-like containers all contained food and there was a letter written in English in one of them.

In that, the Americans told us they would come back every day at a specified time to drop those things we needed most. In the containers was some material which was meant to let them know how many people we had at the camp. We had to line up with 50 people to a row. For every 50, a letter T had to be cut from the material and laid down so the crew would know the amount of supplies needed for their next drop.

Obviously the Americans did not realise there were so many of us as the material was only sufficient for a small number of people.

At that stage most of us were still living in Boskamp. The Americans did come back and Australians had joined them. They dropped more food and we also got more chocolate, which did not melt this time. Then there were apples, prunes, raisins, sultanas and milk powder. They had also included medicines.

Among the food and medicine were notes requesting us to return the parachutes. We had to collect them and return them later but we were disappointed because the material would have made excellent clothes for us.

We could not really blame them for wanting their parachutes back and we were very grateful to the Americans and Australians for all the food they had given us. All the food was distributed honestly by the appointed collectors and everyone was much happier.

One day some American and Australian planes flew over dangerously low. They dropped parcels which came down in the burned-out old camp. They came down at a terrific speed and hit the ground with loud thuds and people who happened to be around dived into the nearest shelters.

The parcels contained army blankets, for which we were very grateful. We had something soft to lie on in our hut – luxury indeed.

The air drops always caused a great commotion because the planes flew over so low making a lot of noise. Children screamed but adults were also affected, me included. It really got on my nerves but the supplies really were friendly fire.

The Japanese were still there and it was amusing to see how they had changed. They were falling over each other in the favour-hunting drive. They gave us sugar, bread, soap and a small number of people – the favoured few – got clothes and shoes. But we were not among those privileged people because the Koning family were no boot-lickers although we knew a few that were.

A minority of women got good clothing and shoes and we never really knew why, although it could have been because they had promised to plea for leniency if Bok'eh was ever brought to trial. There was no way we were going down that road because in our opinion the pig of a commander would deserve all he got.

A few Dutch men from the POW camp at Makassar came to our camp. They did not look well at all, being very thin and malnourished. They had been through hell but they were mobbed by many women and they told us they were organising housing for all of us in Makassar but that it would take some time as most houses were in a terrible mess.

We also had a visit from two men from the Pare Pare civilian men's camp. These two were also mobbed and they too looked thin and old. All the civilian prisoners had suffered badly and many had died. The stories told by these two men were horrendous.

All the sick people, including the dysentery patients, were gradually transported to Makassar. With more and more people leaving, those who had to stay had more food and we were getting well used to a classier diet.

44. Farewell Boskamp, Hello Again to Kampili

At last, the day came when we could leave the hell-hole of Boskamp and move into a new bamboo barrack in Kampili. We had plenty of room now and the well by the barrack contained beautiful clear, cool water. There was even a hand-pump at the well, something only the kitchen well had in the old days. It was sheer luxury and soon we were given sleeping mats and mosquito nets. Bok'eh had gone to live outside the camp and although we hardly ever saw him, he still seemed to be in charge – or at least he thought he was.

We did not get any more plane drops but one day we were visited at the new Kampili barracks by a group of Americans. One of them was a young woman and I thought she was beautiful. She looked as if she had just come from the hairdressers and she had make-up on her pretty face and her lips were painted bright red. She really did make us feel dowdy and unattractive by comparison.

She was wearing a uniform of a khaki-coloured blouse and skirt and she was wearing silk stockings and walked elegantly in a pair of black pumps with medium heels. She was carrying a paper bag full of sweets which she handed out to the children.

I was sitting on one of our bottom bunks when this beautiful creature stopped in front of me. She had a big smile on her lovely face and, holding the bag open to me, she said with an American accent: "Honey, would you like a sweet?" She called me honey. We used to put honey on our bread. I politely refused.

I was ashamed and angry because I was wearing old faded clothes which begged to be thrown away. I was barefooted and my untidy hair was tied together with strips of some shoddy material. My fury was aimed at the Japanese, whose actions had put me in this deplorable situation, prompting a beautiful lady in khaki to offer me a sweet. I was 16 and I know I looked horrible. Looks were not something we could waste our time with but now, with the first people who were not in the same boat as me visiting us and a beautiful lady among them, I was embarrassed. I'd discovered vanity.

The Americans were shown around our awful Boskamp and shook their heads in disbelief. They simply could not understand how we could have lived there and survived. We could see that they tried very hard to hold back the tears. They were very shocked to see the disastrous damage and misery their bombing raids had inflicted on us and they were very sorry indeed.

But, of course, they were not to blame. The Japanese had used us poor defenseless prisoners as a decoy. From the air, all those barracks at Kampili so close to the Japanese ammunition depots and their airfield looked like a military installation – not a concentration camp filled with women and children.

The camp was emptying out quite rapidly now as the Dutch authorities in Makassar were now in charge and had made more houses ready for us.

By the end of September only a small group was left and we were among that minority. It was quite eerie and so very quiet with few people with so much space and not knowing who was guarding us. We did not know it but we were very vulnerable being totally unprotected.

We didn't know it then but in Java there had been an uprising among the Indonesians and they had attacked and killed Dutch prisoners the Japanese were supposed to be protecting now they had lost the war and we didn't need to be guarded any more. I've no idea how the natives saw us because they had suffered just as much, if not more, than us during the war. One thing was certain – there was no way things would ever return to the way they were prior to 1942. The old Dutch East Indies was a thing of the past.

45. Freedom at Last

At last, after what seemed an eternity, at the end of September, our turn came to leave. Trucks with seats arrived to pick us up, which was in stark contrast to the way we had arrived at Kampili two-and-a-half years before. Then it was a high-sided truck with us sitting on the tray bouncing all the way from Malino.

Gathering our pitiful possessions didn't take us long and Leida and I walked around the compound for one last time, which was a strange feeling. We had been there a long time and suffered the deprivation of prisoners and the horror of having bombs dropped on us and the trepidation of a madman for a commandant. We'd seen death and suffering on a monumental scale and seen our tender teenage years turned upside down by an enemy we would never be able to understand. But now we were free and definitely not sorry to be leaving the scene of our captivity.

We came across two cats that had survived. They did not look like strays as they were quite friendly and glad to see us. We picked them up and put them carefully in bags with airholes in them, one cat to a bag. At first they complained a bit but soon settled down and were quiet on our trip back to Makassar.

It was a very hot day and the cruel sun beat down on us as we drove through the gate. We looked back when we hit the road with a sense of relief that we were at last really leaving and driving to that longed-for freedom.

The trip was uneventful and quite relaxing, again in stark contrast to our trip into captivity. When we arrived in Makassar we were driven to a nice house on the corner of two prominent roads. There were already people in the house, who had left Kampili before us. A few of the women were joined by their husbands who had survived the POW camp in Makassar and the civilian camp at Pare Pare.

It was absolutely wonderful to live in a proper house again with a bathroom and toilet, and how heavenly to sleep on a mattress. The committee members who had organised everything such as housing, food distribution, bedding and furniture had really done a marvellous job.

Three times a day a truck from the central kitchen stopped in front of the house to give us food in small wooden barrels rather like meals on wheels. Every day we got meat or fish, vegetables, fruit and rice with plenty of sambal with the main meal. Sambal is a paste made of hot red chillies, onion, sugar, salt and vinegar. It is very healthy and chockful of vitamins and this undoubtedly contributed to the improvement of our health.

Leida and I found out that one of the two cats we brought back from Kampili belonged to the nuns, of which there were about 100 in our camp. So we took the cat to the convent and reunited it with the overjoyed nuns. We kept the other one, as we didn't know who owned it. Unfortunately this animal fell ill and died quickly. There was no vet at the time but the cat died without any distress.

In the back garden of our house there was an air raid shelter and in it lived a brown dog which had had pups. We fed the little dog family and then it started raining and didn't stop for days. The shelter filled with brown muddy water. We waded inside the shelter and rescued the mother and her pups. We dried them off and kept them inside. The bitch had a gammy leg, so we called her Poot (leg of an animal).

There was another dog, a cream coloured bitch with her half-grown pup. We called the bitch Dolly and when walking along the road near the house, Lia witnessed the pup being hit by a jeep, catapulted into a ditch and dying instantly. Lia, largely shielded from some of the grimmer aspects of life at Kampili, was upset for some time by the death of that little dog. Peace time can also be very cruel.

When Poot's beautiful healthy pups were old enough, we found homes for them. Gradually, as the situation returned to as normal as was possible in those early months after the end of the war and more houses were made ready for habitation again, people started to move elsewhere. A single lady living in our crowded house continued to look after the two dogs after we also had to leave.

Mamma received a white postcard and on one side was typed: "We are safe in British hands." Underneath was Pappa's signature and the card was postmarked Batavia (now Jakarta). This was the first evidence that Pappa was really alive. The list at Boskamp was reassuring but this was the real thing and we were overjoyed.

Mamma heard that there were other women whose husbands were in Batavia and they also received the same card with the same message signed by their husbands. We heard then that many men from the POW camp in Makassar had been shipped to Burma where they were forced to work on the infamous Burma railroad. Many had died there. Other men from the camp had been shipped to Japan, where they were forced to work in the mines.

We had no idea, however, when Pappa would be coming back, as there was no communication and transport between the islands. We just had to be patient and wait.

One day, not long after our arrival in Makassar, we were told we could get a free pair of new sandals. It seems a Chinese shoemaker had been shocked to hear the women and children from Kampili had no shoes and had decided to donate a pair of sandals to each of them. He loaded his truck and stationed it in the middle of town and when word got around that sandals were there for the taking, a huge crowd gathered to find their size. We found our pick and were extremely grateful to the shoemaker. We couldn't have paid him even if he had wanted money, because we were penniless.

The sandals were a dream come true, with the uppers made of soft leather so we didn't get blisters on feet that were so unused to having shoes. It was so good to wear something on your feet and I treasured my sandals.

The Japanese had been ordered to clean up the mess left by their occupation. There were many filthy houses and the Dutch authorities wasted no time in getting the Japs to work. In some of the houses the Japs had used rooms as toilets and the filth and decrepid condition of some of these beautiful homes was a real eye-opener. How could they be so revolting?

The Japs were also ordered to clean up the gardens, which would have been beautiful before they arrived with bountiful trees, shrubs and large green lawns. Under the occupation the houses and gardens were totally neglected and overgrown, with most of the plants dead.

We went to the house we lived in before the war and it, like most of the big bungalows, was terribly neglected and the garden was a wilderness. In some rooms, the walls were papered with Japanese newspapers and pictures cut out of Japanese magazines and there was nothing left of our own furniture, clothes or valuables.

It was quite devastating for us. Our beautiful home carried so many happy memories from before the war and now it was just a shell and a smelly dishevelled one at that. The Japs had looted all the European homes and shipped all the valuables to Japan. Pappa had a very valuable and beautiful stamp collection, which was no more and they had burned all our books, photographs and documents. There was no trace left of our having lived in that house.

My beloved piano, which I had pined for when we were living in Malino and had not forgotten at Kampili when other things took on a more important role in the mind of a teenager, was smashed to bits, tossed outside and left to rot upside down under the mango tree. Some people who had witnessed it told us that drunken Japs had kicked the keys off my piano and apparently had great fun vandalising my treasured instrument. What brutes.

The dedicated Kampili teachers, together with those from the different men's camps, banded together and started a school. They had very few educational materials and they received no pay but these amazingly dedicated people only thought of us. We needed education after so long receiving what only amounted to odd snippets and I was very happy to be able to go to school again.

Australian officers and soldiers arrived in Makassar from New Guinea, where they had fought a tough battle against the Japanese under harsh conditions. It had been very difficult for them because New Guinea is a vast island with impenetrable jungles, swift flowing and very wide rivers which flood vast areas during the monsoon and steep, very rocky mountains which are almost always covered with thick layers of snow and ice. The Australians were very pleased to be back in civilisation, even if it was still a rather primitive one which was attempting to rebuild.

We soon made friends with some of the Aussies and they organised dances which were always very orderly, with drunkards immediately thrown out.

Leida and I learned to dance at an Australian social. We used to get picked up by a truck and driven to the dance hall and driven home afterwards and escorted to the door. Everything was conducted in a correct and dignified manner. At that time I was very shy of men and I would only go out if Leida came too and one or more of our Aussie friends I trusted were also present.

I was then 17-years old and I got my first period. I had to lie flat on my back for at least three days bleeding profusely. We could not buy sanitary pads or anything like that because we did not have any money. We only had some rags, which Mamma was forever washing and I thought I was bleeding to death.

At last it stopped but by now I was very weak and remained so for some time. The lateness of my first period is something I can lay firmly at the door of the Japanese but looking back it was probably one of the few blessings of our captivity. Mamma and Leida's periods stopped altogether along with plenty of the other women. But those who continued their regular monthly cycles had a hard time.

It took about six months, when we were in Australia, for my periods to become normal and regular.

46. Reunited at Last

At the end of October, on a very hot afternoon with the sharp sunrays penetrating deep inside the house, Leida and I were disturbed in the middle of some sewing and schoolwork by the sound of a truck which stopped in front of the house.

A man got out of the cabin and the driver, a young Dutchman with a blond crewcut, got out too. They both walked to one side of the truck and the young man lifted a large sack off the back of the lorry and handed it to the older man.

The young crewcut hopped back behind the wheel and drove off, leaving the man walking slowly toward the house carrying the sack.

Leida and I were puzzled by this man coming down our driveway until he came closer. It was Pappa, but he looked very strange and puffy and his head had been shaved.

What great joy. Mamma, Leida, Lia, Pappa and I were together as a family again. Pappa told us that he and a camp-mate had gone to the airport at Batavia and had been living there for quite some time in a large military camp since their transportation from Makassar.

Pappa told us how a tall American POW in the camp next door to his, had come over and told them: "The war is over and that's no bullshit."

Upon release, Pappa and his camp-mate hitched a ride on a freight plane to Balikpapan on Borneo, now called Kalimantan, sitting between the crates of goods. Americans at Balikpapan gave them each a blanket, mosquito net, some clothes, and some cooking pots and a place to pitch a tent they brought from the POW camp.

A ship was soon to leave Balikpapan for Makassar and the two made sure they were on that boat when it left. On arrival at Makassar after two days at sea, they ran into the crew-cutted Dutchman who knew Pappa from the POW camp at Makassar. Then it was home to a different house and getting used to living as a family again.

Pappa was far from well, having been very ill with malaria and still suffering from beri-beri. He had also suffered at the hands of a brutal Japanese guard and was beaten on the head, which left him deaf in one ear for the rest of his life.

We were very happy being together again, living in a proper house and eating three square meals a day. Although our basic needs were taken care of, not everything was quite right yet. We had school but no money, no jobs and no books, something we yearned for after so long being unable to read.

A group of Dutchmen arrived from Holland to organise the administration of all the European people who had survived the war in the Dutch East Indies. The Japs had destroyed all the records, so they had to start from scratch and Mamma was lucky she was able to save the leather handbag with the important papers – a lifeline indeed. But she did not have our birth certificates, so we were interviewed and our names and all the other details were recorded. This was a tremendous task.

We were given some material which was a kind of khaki drill and the clever dressmakers in the family, Mamma and Leida, sewed by hand a nice simple dress for each of us. We were also surprised by the gift of a Red Cross parcel each. Australians and New Zealanders had generously donated to the Red Cross during the war years and the parcels were to help prisoners of war or refugees displaced by the fighting.

We should have had a few parcels each while we were in Kampili but typically, the Japanese never gave them to us. I try and imagine how much of a pick-me-up a Red Cross parcel would have been while we were prisoners in that hellish concentration camp. They could have helped ward off some of the dreadful, deep depressions the women and children all suffered at that camp, or indeed help to end them. What horrible, callous people those Japanese were.

Better late than never, we were delighted to get those parcels. Mine contained a quantity of sky-blue soft wool, a knitting pattern and knitting needles, a beautiful lipstick – my first – and a few other smaller items.

Mamma and Leida had the same things, with the colour of the wool and the patterns being different. Pappa and Lia also got parcels but I can't remember what was in theirs I was so overwhelmed with the excitement of my own.

Mamma taught Leida and me to knit and we immediately started to make our jumpers, which would be totally unsuitable for the Makassar climate, but perfect for the European winter we would encounter when we returned to Holland. I wore my beautiful sky-blue jumper for many years after the war.

47. Struggle for Normality

Although we were free and life returned to as normal as was possible in post- war Makassar, my nightmare was far from over.

Every one of us had tales to tell from the war. It touched everybody. Some heart-breakingly tragic stories emerged and we had all witnessed some of these incredible sob-inducing episodes. They often brought images of pain and suffering into your mind which were impossible to shake off.

As a family, we had suffered but we remained intact, which was more than could be said for so many others. Families broke up after the war with the pressures of family-life becoming too hard to bear after the deprivation and suffering and it was always incredibly sad to hear of divorces between loving couples before the war who had changed as we all had.

My personal horror was claustrophobia and the memory of Kampili haunted me for many years. I had nightmares of the inferno after the bombing raid at the camp on July 17, 1945 and particularly the scene of our burning barrack with Mamma still inside.

War destroys everything that is beautiful and decent. It kills innocent men, women and children and in the end there is nothing left except great misery and desolation – and nobody ever wins.

We were lucky to survive the horrors of that concentration camp but the struggle to survive could have come to nothing but a grim, terrifying end according to documents recently uncovered in the United States. According to these documents, which have the hallmarks of authenticity, in 1944 the commandants of all the Japanese camps received from their government in Tokyo the secret order to execute all prisoners in the event of an American or British invasion. Furthermore, it was to be up to the camp commandants themselves to choose whether they executed their prisoners individually or in groups, and they were also to be free to decide by what method these executions would take place.

This horrible Japanese plan was discovered by the Americans who decoded the orders and even ascertained the date by which this order was to be carried out – August 28, 1945. So it is sobering to think that had the United States not forced Japan to capitulate after dropping the atom bomb on Hiroshima on August 6 and Nagasaki on August 9, none of us would have lived to tell this story and there is no doubt we would have met a grisly end.

The Japs' murderous plan was also the reason the international food-aid action for malnourished prisoners in the camps never came to fruition. The Allied governments and private aid organisations collected nearly 100 million Swiss francs between August 1944 and July 1945. The Dutch government had contributed 2.5 million guilders but not one cent ever reached its destination. We could at least have had some good food in our bellies while we were incarcerated in Kampili and Boskamp but the Japs had pilfered the lot.

48. Bok'eh's Court Martial

On May 22 1946, a short article appeared in the local Makassar paper about the pig Bok'eh's court martial. As we were by this time in Sydney, we heard about it many years later.

The article stated that Yamaji was a war criminal. The next day, May 23, he was due to appear before what was called the Temporary Court Martial, with a Lieutenant-Colonel N.M. Vellenga as chairman and Dr Soumokil the judge.

Bok'eh was accused of having committed a variety of crimes in the men's concentration camp at Pare-Pare and later in the women's and children's camp at Kampili. Numerous accusations had been brought against the man we all hated – or I thought we all hated. In Pare-Pare he had beaten his victims with a split bamboo stick or the handle of a spade. He was also accused of tying a clergyman by his wrists to a crossbar-type thing and hanging him, with his feet not able to touch the ground for some time.

Some of the crimes he had committed against the women at Kampili have been covered but those were only the cruelties I witnessed or had heard about.

He had been almost inhuman when he lost his temper and many women had suffered. And yet, according to the newspaper, Bok'eh had been able to produce a kind of expression of thanks which had been written at some Kampili woman's initiative and had been signed by many others from the camp. According to this document, Yamaji had done a lot to alleviate the hardship and suffering of the women.

We knew absolutely nothing about this document and were never asked if we agreed or wanted to sign it to help save Bok'eh. Had we been, we certainly would have refused and we really didn't believe the assertion that "many other women" would have signed the document for mercy on Bok'eh . There must have been only a very small minority of women whom Bok'eh had favoured for some reason or other who would have signed that despicable document. Others, like us, were furious when we heard that some women had tried to lessen the punishment that Yamaji would have deserved.

A Mrs C.W. Verschoor, a Kampili survivor, wrote a letter to the editor of the paper expressing surprise that Yamaji was accused of having committed the same crimes in Kampili as he had committed in the men's camp at Pare-Pare. She wrote that while there were many things lacking, he had never exercised the brutal Pare-Pare methods on the women at Kampili and stated that Bok'eh (our hate-name that she probably would not have used) had done a lot for the camp. She was sure that many other women would agree with her and there would be many who would not accept the accusations levelled at the commandant.

Mrs Verschoor said it was fair that Yamaji should be punished for the things he was guilty of but repeated that he had done a lot of good at Kampili.

What really got to us in the relative luxury of Sydney in 1946 when we heard of all this, was that this woman Verschoor and the signees of the letter to the courtmartial, have not told us what good Yamaji had done at Kampili. What had he done to alleviate the suffering? Why were we not aware of these acts of kindness from the commandant? How had some obviously been favoured while others had not? What had we done to miss out on the outstretched hands of conciliation that Bok'eh had proferred?

Mrs Verschoor thought that the expression of thanks before the court had been composed totally without pressure, and with the knowledge of the camp leaders, by Kampili internees who became aware on liberation of the exceptionally better treatment they had enjoyed compared with the men. Mrs Verschoor had missed signing the letter of appreciation but stated that she wished to support it in case it was necessary.

She also went on to say that in her opinion the writer of the article had either not been properly informed or had been led by prejudice. She also found it strange that the court action had only been started when most of the witnesses had already left Makassar. She was sure that at that time there were still women who could openly declare that Yamaji had done his utmost for Kampili.

This woman Verschoor is entitled to her views. I didn't know her and had no idea what she did in Kampili. Nor can I understand where she got her ideas from to make all her sweeping statements regarding Yamaji supporters and supposed 'cheerleaders'.

In my opinion, Bok'eh was always thinking of Number One when he gave any concessions at the camp. He was a young Japanese soldier who had power over 1700 women and children. He did his utmost to keep his job because he did not like the possibility of being sent to the battle front. He was irrational, irascible and cruel – nothing less. He was also a consummate coward, which was obvious by the treatment he meted out to the men in Pare Pare before he came to Kampili, the women in our camp and the hapless Dantje, his poor assistant.

That he had supposedly done a lot of good for us is highly debatable and what he had done was with an ulterior motive in mind. He obviously hoped that after the war the Allied powers would be lenient and give him a reduced sentence – or even let him off.

In reply to Mrs Verschoor, the editor wrote that "as far as I am concerned, any Japanese soldier who had beaten women to the ground should be hanged". He added that he doubted whether concentration camp internees could "see things in their normal proportion any more. The Temporary Court Martial was more than capable of handling this case and they, no doubt, had acquainted themselves with what the commandant had done for the women's camp.

"The ladies who were defending Yamaji should really take into consideration that there were many who had suffered very much, so that expressions of sympathy by Dutch women for any Jap cannot be appreciated. In any case, we think it unimportant if this Jap gets a few years more or less."

The note was signed V Vunderink.

All Bok'eh's 'good deeds' and the support of the pariah women did not do him much good. After the court martial there was a brief statement in the newspaper to the effect that the military auditor, whatever he was, had demanded a 10-year jail sentence for the war criminal Yamaji.

I presume Yamaji did get 10 years for his crimes. We heard that after he had completed his jail sentence he returned to Japan. But his freedom was apparently short-lived because, as a rumour went, he was killed in a road accident about four years after his return home.

49. Battles in the Peace

On a very hot, sunny day in March 1946 the Koning family sailed from Makassar on the small ship Curacao for Sydney to recuperate. Among the passengers were people from Kampili, men from the POW camp in Makassar, men from the civilian establishment at Pare Pare and a few Australian soldiers going home.

To qualify for a sojourn in Australia we had to have a thorough medical examination carried out by a doctor especially appointed to the job. Pappa and Mamma had both been very ill with malaria tropica and Pappa still suffered the after-affects of beri-beri. Leida, Lia and I had also been very ill, so we 'qualified' for recuperation in that wonderful country our Aussie friends in Makassar had talked about so much.

Life on board the Curacao was sheer luxury. Leida and I had a cabin to ourselves and Mamma, Pappa and Lia shared the one next to us.

One young Australian soldier made friends with us. He was a nice, well-mannered young man and was like a brother to Leida, Lia and me.

Off the north-eastern Australian coast we hit a storm and as the small boat had nothing in its holds, we rolled and pitched and were tossed about like a cork. In the pantry there was a shocking mess, with jam, sugar, flour and anything else that was contained in a jar or tin all mixed together in a disgusting concoction and sloshing around on the stomach-churning movements of the ship.

We were greatly relieved when we sailed into Townsville. The Curacao berthed at the end of a very long pier and as we all went ashore the ship was fumigated to kill the many rats and mice living in the empty holds and coming up in search of food.

Our young Australian friend came with us. There was no public transport from the pier to the town but we managed to get a lift on a truck. Sitting on the open tray we were driven to the town and delivered to a hotel, whose management had been asked to receive us, let us freshen up, use the comfortable lounge and provide refreshments and lunch.

We had several hours till lunchtime and the young Aussie offered to show us Townsville. We were full of admiration for the small town. What a lovely place nestled between the foot of a mountain and the blue sea.

Pappa had received some money from the Dutch government, so we decided to replace the well-worn sandals provided by the generous Chinese shoemaker in Makassar with some proper shoes. We bought a pair each, which separated Pappa from quite a bit of his money, the first pay he had received in four years.

The hotel gave us a lovely lunch and afterwards we sat in the lounge and talked before we had to return to the ship. Later that afternoon our voyage to Sydney continued, minus the pests, and we had good weather for the trip down the coasts of Queensland and New South Wales. Then at last we quietly sailed into Sydney's beautiful harbour.

We were all very excited and before disembarking we were quickly examined, by doctors who looked at our hands and skin. I don't know what they were looking for but we obviously passed with flying colours. Then there were forms to be completed, checks made about our identity and coupons to buy clothes as rationing was still in operation.

Arrangements had been made for our accommodation and transport and we said goodbye to our fellow passengers, members of the crew and to our young Australian friend. I can't remember his name and we never saw him or heard from him again.

We were driven to a house in Dee Why, where Miss Francis lived with her elderly mother. Miss Francis was very nice and really looked after us very well. Mamma and Pappa had a bedroom inside while Leida, Lia and I slept on the enclosed verandah.

It was very peaceful there and we enjoyed the good food, the clean air and occasional swim at Dee Why beach. We soon made friends and our best friend was Joan Cobb, who lived in Dee Why. Leida and I spent many hours with Joan and her friendly parents. Joan still lives in Dee Why and over the years we have kept in touch.

We were very excited at being able to buy new clothes and seemed a million miles and light years away from the rags we had to wear in Kampili and Boskamp.

There were a lot of Dutch people in Sydney and among them were teachers who got together and hired a dance hall at Milsons Point under one end of the Sydney Harbour Bridge. They started a high school and we were taught in English from English text books. I loved that school and Sydney fascinated me. I particularly enjoyed sitting on the ferry and gently sailing across the harbour, the bus rides, going to the pictures, the crowds in the city and visits to the zoo.

The board we paid Miss Francis was rather high, so Mamma and Pappa decided to rent a flat in Manly, which was closer to the city and therefore cheaper for travel.

Lia soon found children her age to play with and one day I was doing my homework in the living room when I heard a shrill little voice echo up from the street below: "Shut up you dirty little cow." I went down to investigate and it had been my little sister who had shouted. She had picked up the local lingo already.

While we were in Sydney and getting ready to leave for Holland, we met a woman who was involved in recruiting nurses for the big hospital in the city. She suggested Leida and I stay in Sydney and train to be nurses, which she thought we would be very good at.

We turned her down because we had only recently been reunited as a family after four years apart and I wanted to finish high school because I thought I was so far behind. Besides, physically and psychologically I was not up to any strenuous nursing training.

I felt very insecure and inadequate and both Leida and I couldn't bear the thought of Mamma, Pappa and Lia leaving us in Australia to go to the other side of the world. I do not regret our decision to turn down the opportunity to be a nurse, although I did try some years later.

After a wonderful stay in Sydney we had to leave and say goodbye to all the friends we had made. We left in October 1946 and the sea journey on a passenger liner that had been converted to a troop carrier was far from comfortable – a vast difference to the little ship Curacao we had arrived in. In the bow, a large section had been converted to a big dormitory with rows of hammocks and the men slept in these. Pappa said that if the ship rocked, even slightly, the hammocks bumped into each other, making sleeping very difficult. It was also very hot and stuffy.

The women and children were accommodated in large dormitories down below. There were canvas beds in lots of four and Mamma, Leida, Lia and I had one such foursome. There was not much room between the four beds, which were covered with a cotton underlay and had no mattresses, just a pillow and blanket. There were toilets and very small shower boxes with cold seawater and tiny basins set into the hull of the boat, so they were quite cramped.

Part of the crew were male Dutch university students who were employed to wash dishes, clean showers, toilets and kitchens as well as serve at the tables.

There were so many Dutch people from Japanese camps on board that there was a shortage of domestic help. Leida and I were among teenagers asked if we wanted a paid job – the first time we had worked for money. It wasn't much but it was our own.

We had to clean our dormitories, showers and toilets as well as take turns to wash and dry the dishes. Leida and I were disgusted to see the students having fun throwing dishes through the portholes in the kitchen. Like a game of darts, one would stand a short distance from a porthole with a stack of plates. To get a bullseye a plate had to go through the porthole and into the sea and a loud hurrah greeted each success. Of course, quite a number of efforts didn't make it to the sea and crashed to the floor in pieces. Leida and I never played the game but there was nobody to stop it and a lot of the ship's crockery met a watery end.

Working in the steamy, airless dormitories soon caused me to have fainting spells. Mamma took me to the ship's doctor, who told Mamma that I must not work any more and should rest and sit on the deck in the fresh air as much as possible.

I really felt terrible and looked very pale. A nice maths teacher from Java always came to sit with us on deck and he gave me lessons, which was fantastic, as maths was not my strong point.

After many weeks at sea we finally arrived at a very wintry, bleak looking Amsterdam. It was dreadfully cold with an icy wind that blew right through our coats.

None of our relatives could accommodate us, so we were packed in a bus and driven to a repatriation centre in Noordwijk, a beach resort. Mamma, Leida, Lia and I had to share a room with a handful of other women and we were back to the all-too familiar top and bottom bunks. Our bedroom was stuffy and hot and with air conditioning, we could not open a window.

One old woman snored all night like the engine of a motorboat and I also had a blocked nose so that sleeping was almost impossible. Poor Pappa had to sleep in the attic, again in a hammock which we thought was a bit unfair.

During the years in Kampili I often wondered what it would be like to have a room all to myself. It was an impossible dream then, of course, but I had come close when we sailed from Makassar to Sydney when I had just Leida to share with. But the sea journey to Holland had been horrendous and this dormitory was just as bad.

I had had my own room once. When we moved to Makassar and rented our home on the Hospitaalwag I luxuriated in my own bedroom – but that was in 1941, so it was a short-lived luxury before the move to Malino and then Kampili where there was no privacy at all.

On our return to Holland we thought the Dutch authorities' attitude to us was poor and we did not feel at all welcome. We had suffered as Dutch people in a Dutch colony and while we knew the people in the Netherlands had suffered terribly with the German occupation, we thought our treatment 'back home' was poor.

At that time Holland had a Labour government and it was red as hell. When they were timidly and politely asked if there was any compensation coming for losing our freedom and everything we possessed and being ill-treated by a brutal enemy, they asked why we were complaining. We were told we had a roof over our heads and were fed. Beggars can't be choosers, we were told. We heard later that the authorities had been disappointed that so many of us had come back.

After a short stay at the Noordwijk repatriation centre during which we met our relatives, we were sent to the northern province of Friesland, where the people speak a Fries dialect which we could not understand.

We were accommodated in a tiny village called Sint Nikolaasga, where there were already some people who had come straight from the Dutch East Indies. Mamma, Pappa and Lia got a room downstairs with central heating, while Leida and I had to sleep in the attic, a large empty space which had been converted into little bedrooms with cardboard partitions, one of which was reserved for Leida and me. Our bedroom contained two wooden cots with straw mattresses but nothing else but a small window which gave a view over the beautiful garden of the home. In the hall there were a few basins which all the cardboard room occupants had to use.

After all those years living in the tropics of the Dutch East Indies, we were hit by a record cold winter in 1946-47 and Leida and I could not sleep for the cold. It was so cold that thick ice formed on the inside of the little bedroom windows. The most difficult thing to keep warm were our feet. The water pipes froze so it was just as well Mamma and Pappa's room had hot and cold water so we could have a wash there.

We were treated like sick people. We always had to drink hot milk which, by the time it was cool enough to drink, had a thick yellow skin on the top. The milk was served in beakers which had chipped rims and while I was grateful for the milk, putting the chipped rims to our mouths worried us, as we were afraid we'd catch some contagious disease.

Leida and I sometimes went for a walk in the village. One day when we were walking along the cobblestone street, the children streamed out of the village school at the end of the school day. They were wearing wooden clogs, which made a lot of noise on the cobblestones.

A few of the kids spotted us and in no time we had all the children clomping after us. One child said: "Look at those women, they are wearing pants." Leida and I were wearing the woollen slacks we had bought in Sydney. We felt very embarrassed and rushed back to the home with the little monsters running after us till they could go no further and all the while shouting and attracting the attention of villagers, who appeared everywhere staring at us.

We were pleased to leave that home. Our next accommodation was in Leeuwarden at the home of a lovely widow, Mrs Hofman. We lived upstairs, where there was a second kitchen so that Mamma could cook our own meals.

I went to the high school in Leeuwarden but did not like it very much. Although I had had some schooling in Kampili and Sydney, I was still behind. But I wasn't alone, as there were other people from Japanese camps on Java who were in the same boat as me. The teachers gave us extra lessons at night so we could catch up and though it was pretty tough, I was grateful to the teachers for giving up their time and their homes to push us along.

At the school there were many farmers' sons and daughters who wore clogs. When they got to school they would step out of the clogs and line them up on the floor under their coats which were hanging on pegs. From the row of clogs on the floor there was a nauseating odour that spread along the corridor on the ground floor. Thankfully, the classroom I was in was upstairs, where the smell was less.

Pappa had to return to the Dutch East Indies and was posted again to Bandoeng on Java. Mamma and Lia went to join Pappa after I had sat and passed my exams. I went to live in Leiden in a kind of boarding house and I commuted by train to The Hague where I attended a secretarial course at Schoevers. At the end of the year-long course I passed the exams and was presented with the diploma. While I was living in Leiden, Leida went to live in Haarlem and became a dressmaker and also studied embroidery.

In 1950 I started work at an international shipping company in Rotterdam in the accountancy department and rented an attic flat in the heart of the city, which had been extensively damaged by bombing during the war. When I moved there large parts of the port were still in ruins. They had started the monumental task of clearing the rubble away, leaving vast barren spaces.

Although I had a good job I got sick of people, the real busybodies, trying to run my life and trying to marry me off. There were a number of bachelors but I did not like them and the thought of having to spend the rest of my life cooped up in some small apartment in a high-rise building with a husband and kids appalled me. Of course these people meant well but they were too much for me.

An exception to this rule was my friend from Malino Lily Schiphorst, who was a nurse in Rotterdam and we roomed together in a pension for a time when I first moved to the city. She met her husband, who was a photographer at a beach resort not far from Rotterdam and she moved away. I had a room to myself again for the second time in my life. I caught up with Lily again in 1958 when I returned to Holland and she persuaded me I would make a good nurse. I thought it wasn't a bad idea because I was getting a bit sick of working in offices and if I qualified, I could always go back to Australia.

But it wasn't to be. By now I was 30 and had to share a room with three other women who were much younger than me and that definitely did not work, even though they were very nice girls. Basically the age difference was difficult and with the rigorous discipline applied at the hospital, I decided I wasn't cut out for nursing. I couldn't cope with being around sick and dying people again.

In 1952, my dear grandmother – Mamma's mother – passed away. I had visited her often when I had been living in Leiden and attending college at The Hague. Some months after her death, with the situation in Asia deteriorating and the Dutch East Indies having gained independence to become Indonesia, Pappa decided on early retirement, so Mamma, Pappa and Lia returned to Holland.

The Indonesians had suffered terribly during the war from the Japanese brutality. Their livelihoods had often depended on us but with the Dutch out of the picture it was difficult to see how some of the natives survived.

I remember one time in March 1944 an Indonesian policeman brought into the camp some natives he had accused of being thieves. Yamaji set to beating them up and then invited the policeman to have a go at thrashing his compatriots.

Another punishment meted out to Indonesians who were accused of stealing was for the alleged thieves' hands and feet to be tied together and then they were tied to a tree. In the trees lived giant ants which would bite the hapless captives. I don't know whether any of the Indonesians died from that treatment but if they did I cannot imagine a worse death.

Many of the Indonesians turned on the Dutch during the war. These people were probably glad that the colonial masters were suffering at the hands of the Japanese. There were plenty of loyal natives but the Japanese terrorised them out of showing any such loyalty and there were brutal punishments if they were caught helping us.

The push for Indonesian independence had begun well before the war with plenty of help from a Japanese man called Nishijima Shigitada, who arrived in Batavia (Jakarta) in 1937. He had been a student at university in Tokyo but was expelled because it was alleged he had communist sympathies.

Shigitada studied both the Dutch and Indonesian languages and got a job in the Chioday Department Store in Bandoeng, although all the time he was employed by the Japanese Information Service. He was a spy and Shigitada had many friends in the fledgling independence movement. His most important companion was Ahmed Soebardjo Djojoadisoerio, who had studied law at Leiden University in the Netherlands. He was to become minister of foreign affairs in the new Republic of Indonesia.

The Japanese worked hard at destabilising the Dutch East Indies and kept at it during the war. In 1944 a school – Asrama Indonesia Merdeka – was founded at which youths aged 18 years and older were trained to take up certain posts in an independent Indonesia. The director of the school was Mr Soebardjo, while the Japanese were in charge of the daily management. Lectures were given by persons like Sukarno, who was to become the first president of an independent Indonesia.

After the war the movement grew from strength to strength, particularly in the general mayhem and uncertainty of the political situation after the Japanese were defeated. The movement was also aided by the British, under pressure at the clamour for independence in India, who had been sent to the Dutch East Indies to take over from the Japanese. They generally lorded it over the Dutch and seemed to order them about. Lord Louis Mountbatten was Commander-in-Chief of the Allied Military Forces.

Sukarno had in the meantime proclaimed an independent Indonesia and the red and white flag was hoisted on August 17, 1945. The Dutch troops on Malacca and in Singapore, (who were former POWs) were not allowed to land on Java under the orders of Mountbatten and the Dutchmen under the command of van Mook, who had come from Australia, did not arrive in Batavia until the beginning of October.

Meanwhile, Indonesian youths had taken possession of the streets and the turbulent times after the Japanese capitulation led to many deaths. While the British, aided by the power of sea, air and land troops maintained order in Singapore and Malacca, on Java many innocent civilians met their deaths as the independence movement struggled to wrest control.

By the end of 1946 order in the former Dutch East Indies was again restored and in November 1946 the British left. Mountbatten had made Sukarno an offer to make the Republic of Indonesia a member of the British Commonwealth, which was rejected.

For The Netherlands, the case was clear. It was now only a question of time before they lost complete control of their colony. While the Dutch hung on grimly over the next three years in the face of a crippled Indonesian economy and a rampant independence movement, on December 27, 1949, our Queen Juliana signed the resolution to grant independence.

The sovereignty transfer went very smoothly but the United States of Indonesia had a very short life. In June 1950, that agreement was torn up and the Republic of Indonesia, which had been declared with Japanese aid way back in August 1945, had become a reality.

Soon after Mamma, Pappa and Lia's arrival back, I decided to emigrate to Australia. Friends of ours who were living there had invited me to stay with them and I had no problem getting all the emigration documents, a medical examination and a chest x-ray. The Australian government even paid my passage.

I felt terrible leaving Pappa, Mamma, Lia and Leida, who by this time was married to Wim, an architect and had one child, Bart. Leida later had Reijer, then Kees, who died of an asthma attack aged 15, Louisa, who is now living in Oregon and Ernst.

My ship sailed from Amsterdam on a grey, very cold, wet and windy day at the end of 1952. On board were Dutch, Belgian and German emigrants and it was a pleasant voyage. There were 10 young women in our cabin, nine single Dutch women and one married woman from Germany, and most were heading to Melbourne.

My friends were waiting for me at the wharf in Melbourne to take me to their home, which was only a bach in the middle of nowhere. There was no way I could get a job there, so I hitchhiked back to Melbourne and shared a flat with Rie, a cabin mate from Holland.

Rie became engaged before she came to Australia and Wim, her fiance, was living in a hostel for men in Melbourne. I soon found a job and Rie was married with me as her bridesmaid. Life was a whirl and I was very happy – I had a room to myself and that luxury I had for many years.

I had made many friends of different nationalities and I joined the Dutch folk dancing group, which joined other groups from other countries in charity performances and once a year we all participated in the Moomba Festival. We walked, each group in their national costume, through the heart of the city, ending up at the Town Hall. We Dutch dancers all wore wooden clogs. It was really tough walking a long way in them, but we attracted a lot of attention.

One day we were invited to dance on television, which had just come into the country.

Eventually all my friends married and I didn't like any of the single men I met, so in 1958, aged 30, I decided to return to Holland. Pappa had bought a new house in a new housing development in a small place called Huizen, not far from Hilversum but getting a job in Holland after having lived six years in Australia turned out to be very frustrating and disappointing. It was then that I tried my abortive attempt at becoming a nurse.

During the long sea voyage from Melbourne to Southampton, I met a young Dutch woman, Rikie, who was going on holiday to the Netherlands Antilles from Auckland, New Zealand and we kept in touch.

I still found Holland too stifling for me and again the busybodies were trying to run my life and attempted match-making was the bane of my life. So I contacted Rikie and told her I wanted to emigrate again, to New Zealand this time. Again I had no difficulty in obtaining the necessary documents, although I had to pay my own way.

I arrived in Auckland in February 1960 and I moved in with Rikie in a flat in Remuera – another room to myself! I had no problem getting a job and at that time I found New Zealand beautiful, peaceful, green and clean with plenty of space – a far cry from Holland. Like Indonesia, I saw houses with big gardens full of beautiful trees and flowers, with well-kept lawns.

In December 1960 I met my husband Oliver and we were married in July 1961. Lia had emigrated to New Zealand before the wedding so she could be my bridesmaid. I no longer had a room to myself but I did not mind sharing then!

We lived in the coalmining town of Huntly in the Waikato for some time and have two sons Paul, 36, a nurseryman and Mark, 35, an aircraft engineer in Los Angeles.

In December 1966 Mamma and Pappa emigrated to New Zealand and lived in Auckland for more than 30 years, while Leida stayed in Haarlem and has four children and nine grandchildren.

I lived a peaceful life as a suburban housewife in Auckland with two growing boys. I had stopped moving and was having what could be called the first normal period of my life since 1941. My sons grew up and in 1979 I set out to achieve what the war and the Japanese had denied me. I went to Selwyn College night classes in the nearby suburb of Kohimarama and studied University Entrance German and English. I passed and decided to go to university and study for a Bachelor of Arts and studied German and Indonesian. I graduated with a BA in 1987 from the University of Auckland, completed Indonesian to stage three in 1988 and in 1989 started studying for a Master of Arts.

This I got with honours in 1992 after writing a thesis on pre-war Indonesian poetry. I would then have liked to have gone on for a PhD but decided I couldn't afford it.

I had achieved what was a long-held ambition – to go to university. I had done that secretarial course in Leiden all those years ago because I couldn't afford university, but I had not really liked that kind of work. I often think what might have been but really, I am just so happy that my ambition was at last fulfilled.

I have been asked whether I would like to go back to Indonesia and see the places I grew up in and even to find any trace of Kampili. My answer is an emphatic no. Apart from all the violence that has been wracking the country in recent times, I want to remember Indonesia as it was, when it was the Dutch East Indies, and it was my home. My childhood memories are still with me, but unfortunately the memories of my teenage years have tended to cloud them. Thank you, Japan, for nothing.

Epilogue

While being held prisoner in a concentration camp, we suffered physically, emotionally and psychologically and was deprived of every human right. We suffered natural disasters, horrific bombing, hunger and sickness. There was great sadness, tragic deaths, inconsolable grief, stress and anguish. Basically there was every form of human suffering imaginable.

Now, after all these years the memory has surfaced very clearly. I am still suffering and I don't think this will ever diminish. Now that my memory is clearer and I feel confident to write in the English language, I decided to write this account.

My intention is to let people, particularly the young, know what life was like in a Japanese concentration camp. Also, how we coped in very difficult circumstances and coped because we believed that one day the nightmare would end and our lives would return to normal again.

I want to show the courage of the women in our camp with their hard work and the dedication of our teachers. And I hope that people will realise that love, decency, honesty, tolerance and understanding are the most important things in life.

War does not achieve any of these things. War only brings death, destruction and incredible misery. War is only to satisfy someone's greed for power. They are the ones who live in luxury far from the battles being fought by their subjects who have been indoctrinated into believing that in the end they will be better off. War also benefits industrialists who make the machinery of war at vast profits. As long as we allow dictators and their cronies and henchmen to rule, there will never be peace and happiness in this world.

Mamma and Pappa were happily married for 71 years. They were modest, honest and selfless people and wonderful parents to Leida, Lia and myself. During the 1930s' depression years, Pappa's salary was cut by 25 percent but they managed and never complained. Pappa was grateful that he still had a job. Thousands of Dutchmen in the Dutch East Indies lost their jobs and had to return to Holland. During those years before Lia was born, Mamma and Pappa made great sacrifices because Leida and I always came first.

Although Pappa's income was never very high, we lived a happy and good life till the Japanese invasion and occupation shattered it. We were lucky to have survived and start a new life.

In The Netherlands the Stichting Japanese Ereschulden – Foundation for Japanese Honorary Debts – known as JES was founded during 1990. The staff consists of former POWs and internees, men and women. They printed claims forms and sent them to every former prisoner of the Japanese. We all completed our forms and returned them to JES head office at The Hague.

Over the years these beautiful volunteers have worked tirelessly for the cause of putting pressure on the Japanese government to apologise and to compensate all the people they held prisoner.

We give an annual donation and receive the JES news magazine four times a year, which keeps us up to date with the case. Once a year they have a donors' general meeting in Holland.

Some JES staff members have visited Tokyo on a number of occasions and have managed to get eight Japanese lawyers to take up their case. During these visits they have also been interviewed by Japanese television and newspaper reporters, which helps to make the Japanese people know what really happened during the war. Apparently, the Japanese people they spoke to were shocked at the stories from the war.

In November 1998, the JES delegates and their eight Japanese lawyers went to court. There were also delegates from Australia, Britain, the United States and New Zealand. The tension was high. Would the Japanese government at last admit wrongdoing and agree to compensate us? The JES and their allied friends were full of hope.

The Japanese judge walked in, sat down and told them there was no compensation. Case closed after only a few minutes and the judge left the court room.

During the years since the war, many of the prisoners of the Japanese have passed away, including my dear parents. But JES is not giving up. Some of them, who had put in everything, have also died and I believe it is very noble and courageous for the JES people to continue to fight our case while there is really very little hope of a favourable outcome.

But no-one should ever forget how many thousands of prisoners and internees – men, women and children of different nationalities – were tortured and starved and are still suffering psychologically and bearing scars that probably will never properly heal, as mine haven't. And we should never forget all those thousands of innocent people who have died.

I believe that the majority of Japanese people are unaware of the horror and brutality the members of the Imperial Japanese armed forces were responsible for during World War 2. The women left behind in Japan had no idea and the generations since have been denied all knowledge because of the censorship, and in some cases the rewriting, of the history books. The worst war criminals were described as real heroes and the Japanese war machine contributed to a glorious period in the country's history. They lost, but my word, they made so many people suffer on the path to their ultimate defeat.

I do not hate the Japanese people. How can one hate a nation that has been kept in the dark for so long about the truth and horror of that war? The terrible irony of it is, however, that successive generations of ignorant Japanese are going to have to face up to the continued ire of the thousands that suffered at the hands of their fathers and grandfathers. I am hopeful that one day the generation of the new millennium will apologise fully and beg our forgiveness.